D1525094

START LIVING YOUR BEST LIFE NOW

4/2/15

To: Ms. Parhams

Never Change, Never Stop,
Never bend & Never Break!!
Your smile, your perspective & your
way is needed by the world...
I am because we are — Ubunti
I hope this serves as proof
That you made a difference.
Your love, your support &
your encouragement helped
me to be who I am!

Love
Ronnella
AKA
Realism
H.

START LIVING YOUR BEST LIFE NOW

7 WAYS TO BEGIN CREATING YOUR DESIRED REALITY

REALISM HARGRAVE

EDITED BY FRANK J. MILES

REALISM HARGRAVE COMMUNICATIONS

Published by Realism Hargrave Communications

ISBN: 978-0-615-93851-6

Edited By Frank J. Miles
Logo Design Juan Beras
Cover Design by Benjamin Davis
Cover Photography by Charles Mitchell
Author Website www.realismhargrave.com

Typesetting services by BOOKOW.COM

Start Living Your Best Life Now is Dedicated
To my Beloved Family
Gregory Hargrave (my husband, my best friend,
my #1 investor), Biasia Young (my daughter, my
everything) and Shameek Hargrave (my son, my
pride and joy) – It is my greatest prayer that you
all Start Living Your Best Life Now, throughout
every second, every minute, and every hour of each
day for the rest of your lives.
To my Mother
Dorothy Bynum-Walker (my mama real, my #1
fan) –I thank you for everything you have done for
me and you are my greatest shero. I wish that I
am at the very least half of the woman that you
are. All that I do, I do it in honor of you.
To my Siblings
Roy Bynum (my chef, my good time), the Rev.
Isis Walker-Harris (my rock, my twin), Marla

Walker (my diary, my heart), Antoinette Olius (my princess, my sister/daughter), and Mark Olius (my little big brother, my main man) —Each of you have always been my greatest motivation. "I am because we are." — Ubuntu.

To my Friend

Michael Thomas (my muse), —We are here at this time because of you as I have never been challenged and impacted greater by another human being. For better or worse your energy has awakened me and I thank you kindly.

To You

The Reader (my reason), —It is my hope that you extract an understanding that there is no need to wish that your life were differently, when you have the power to make it different. If you believe it, then you can absolutely achieve it.

I have risen from very humble beginnings, as the middle child of seven to a single mother living in Urban America to exciting career paths as an Entrepreneur, a Media Personality, a Photographer, and a Humanitarian. Through these careers and a lot of old-fashioned elbow grease, I have been afforded a multitude of opportunities to interact with those whom are said to be great. From the local who's who in my adopted hometown of Newark, New Jersey, like Senator Cory Booker, to big name celebrities like Russell Simmons, Soledad O'Brien, Michael Strahan, Marsha Ambrosius, Shaquille O'Neal, Susan Taylor, Dr. Michael Eric Dyson, the Rev. Jesse Jackson, and many others. Now this all seemed to be a dream come true, until I realized that these exciting careers were the very things that were blocking me from living my ideal life.

Sure, it was great to interview P. Diddy, have fashion icon June Ambrose fawn over my stylish ways, have the inside scoop on the Whitney Houston funeral, be recognized in my community as an asset and have former Newark Mayor Cory Booker acknowledge my contributions to the city by introducing me and blowing me up to one of my sheros, Gayle King (one person away from Oprah, I almost died). However, on the other side of my grass; I wasn't spending any time with my family and friends; my marriage, or rather love life, was in severe trouble; I was overworked and underpaid; I wasn't taking care of my health; I was completely overwhelmed with the issues in my community; I was always in a rush, feeling as if there were never enough hours in the day; I wasn't exploring the other things I've always wanted to do, and to make matters worse – I was spiritually starved.

Being on the scene at the scene when the scene was being seen became a huge distraction to everything else important in my life, besides my children and the ailing feeling that there was a need for change. The cost of success made me realize that I didn't really want success; I wanted freedom. Therefore, I was completely happy and completely unhappy at the same time! I thought I was doing everything right; go to school, get a job, start a business, get married, have children, give back, go to church, and be loving and kind. In spite of doing all of those things and being recognized as well as appreciated for my work, I secretly felt somewhat like a fraud.

By that I mean, when you are a leader, go-to person or highly recognized, people begin to forget you're human and they treat you like you have it all together. Then most times, you get trapped in that false reality because you are now someone's Great Symbol of Hope! For me, I was lacking a work-life balance, and I made life-changing commitments at an early age before I really had a great understanding of who I truly was. Like many others, there were parts of my life that were going absolutely well and then there were parts that were going completely wrong. That's when I started to think about what my ideal life really looked like.

I desired a life of balance, a life where all aspects worked cohesively with one another rather than in competition, a life where I could be my absolute self, a life with healthy and mutually beneficial relationships, a life free of struggle and violence, a life where I could spend leisure time with my family and friends, a life that pushed me to explore and conquer, a life where others contributed to me just as much as I did them, a life where I was simultaneously spiritually, physically, mentally, and emotionally well. So being the doer that I am, I immediately began to search for possibilities to shift my life and its priorities into the direction of my true happiness. That's when I noticed; it wasn't just me!

Everywhere I looked there were both prominent and not so prominent folks who were living life by default, and secretly desiring more. These individuals were being imprisoned by the life they were living now and the life they so desperately wanted to live. So, I pondered on it. I began to think about all of the greats I came in contact with. I reflected upon the conversations about the cost of success, how they felt alone in the world because everyone looked up to them, and the common sentiment that life was one big juggling act, where you had to constantly lose simply to gain every now and again. All of the pretending and superficial aspects of everyday life was strangling those who really just wanted to be happy; ultimately all of us.

I discovered in our quest to seek happiness that we all were being controlled by the false ideals of what it actually was. Everything we do is motivated to capture or provide happiness for self and the ones we love. When we fail to deliver this happiness, we begin to succumb to the ideals of it rather than understand that our happiness is personal and specific. Happiness is not a one-size-fits-all campaign. Upon realizing these revelations, I also acknowledged that it was extremely imperative for each of us to do something to change this underserved but universally and unconsciously agreed-upon perspective of living.

This newfound understanding made a profound influence upon my way of thinking as I suddenly changed my perspective, and therefore I changed my entire reality. I began to immediately transform my life, and in a matter of a few short months, I was happier than I had ever been before, and operating in a way that pleased me greatly as well as one that was in alignment with my true nature. I accomplished this by doing what was best for me at the time, which was taking some much-needed time off and radically detoxifying my life. I relocated from New Jersey to the Greater Atlanta Area; I ended tumultuous relationships; and I left money, recognition, access, influence, and prominent projects on the table. I surrendered to the process of rigorous soul-searching, and I was compelled to write this book, "Start Living Your Best Life Now: 7 Ways to Begin Creating Your Desired Reality."

What you will find in this book is the necessary understanding on how to stop doing what you are doing now, and to start doing what you wish. I use my own personal story as your frame of reference to put a human face and experience on the decisions and choices that you must make to begin living your best life now. I walk you through my thinking, my perceptions, and my understanding as it unfolded in my very own life. You will feel the intensity of my honesty, you will relate to my hardships, you will recognize yourself through me, and you will be challenged to obtain the courage to live, to think, to be, to do, and to serve. The quotes at the beginning of each chapter are taken directly from one-on-one interviews between the personality quoted and myself. When I began writing "Start Living Your Best Life Now," I really had no idea on what I would actually say, so I allowed this book to write itself. This is the entire framework of the "Start Living Your Best Life Now" ideal. You must relinquish control, and allow your internal consciousness to guide you throughout your life.

"Start Living Your Best Life Now" is for people who wish things in their lives were different.

Acknowledgements

First & Foremost all Glory must go to God as without God there is none of us! I thank God for using me as an instrument within his will. As I myself am nothing more than a simple messenger. Each person listed below has contributed to my growth and development in their own unique way and for that I am grateful and I thank you all.

{FAMILY} -Ronnell Walker, Sheila & Janie Singletary, Helen Watson, Elizabeth Hargrave, Elizabeth Foreman, James C. Foreman III, Nicole Wilkerson, Lawrence Young, Yakima Thomas, Haneesah Brown, Hafeezah Brown, Geneva Brown Shiron Hargrave, Dawn Callaway, Shakira Young, H. Monique Williams, Corey Harris, Sharon & Robin Barnes, All of my nieces and nephews from the Bynum, Walker, Olius, Hargrave, Young, Watson, Thomas, Brown, Foreman, Callaway & Wilkerson families & my God baby.

{FRIENDS} -Malikah Coleman, Naomi Scott, Tabilah Austin, Latoya Hendricks, Ebony Smith, Tosha Thomas, Kareesha Cook, Tameeka Arnold, Safiyyah Muhammad, Shalise Day, Muslimah Baldwin, Kat Torres, Darnitah Moultrie, Muhammad Coles, Yucef Mayes, Tumba Cool, Jaleem Johnson, Omar Townes, Shariff James and Dilettante Bass

{HONORABLE MENTIONS} -Mrs. MaryAnn Cool, Ms. Janet Parhams, Ms. Grace Cook, Mrs. Deborah Sykes-Vaughn, Mrs. Cheryl Malone-Brown, Ms. Michelle Murchison, Dr. Akil Khalfani, Frank Miles,

Ebot Pascal Ako, Ronnella Kengne Ako Ebot, Mikki Enix, DamitaJo Morse, Shaniq Garner, Elite Radio, Ky Williams, Mr. & Mrs. Henry & Genise Austin, Deborah Ferdinand, Jacqueline Moore, The city & people of Newark, NJ

It is tragic how few people ever "possess their souls' before they die. "Nothing is more rare in any man," says Emerson, "than act of his own." It is quite true. Most people are other people. Their thoughts are someone else's opinions, their lives a mimicry, their passions a quotation[...]. God has far more pity for the rich, for the hard hedonist, than for those who waste their freedom in becoming slaves to things[...]. To live for others as a definite self-conscious aim was not his creed[...].

-OSCAR WILDE

Contents

CHAPTER ONE

DESIRE A DIFFERENT REALITY

"You have to think about your story, and what you want to attract in your life? You have to be all that you desire, if you expect to ever obtain it."

June Ambrose, Celebrity Stylist and Fashion Icon

When the urge to change my life became completely unbearable to continue ignoring, I was completely displaced. I knew things were not right, but I had no idea how to make them better. At first, I thought that I just needed to do more of what I was already doing. I believed that if I could just speed up the successes and make more money then I would obtain the time and flexibility to do all the other things that I wanted to do. I imagined that this formula would increase the actual quality of my overall life, which is what I desired so greatly. For some of you, dependent upon where you currently are; you're probably feeling the same way.

Playing tug of war with different ideas such as; I hate this job, but it pays the bills, so I am going to continue going to it. I have my bachelor's degree; I'm not getting enough money, and I am thinking about going back to school to pursue a master's degree. I'm most fulfilled serving the community, but I am going to have to stop because I need to make money. The business is not doing so well, so I am going to shut it down and start a new business or go back to school. I'm doing this or that and I hate it. I can't do what I really want because I don't have the money. Or, I'm working one job and I need to go acquire another because the more money I have the more I can do and the happier I will be.

Sorry to bust your bubble but none of those displaced ideals is going to get you there! Matter of fact, that type of thinking will push you further away from what you really want. The reason being is because money is not the key to happiness; nor does it buy it. I know what you're thinking; "what are you telling me, more money in my life is not going to make me happy?" Yes, that's exactly what I'm telling you. If you refuse to believe that you might as well close this book right now, as it's not for you at this time. Money is a powerful resource, but in our quest for it something happens to us. We lose ourselves! We begin to judge our lives, our efforts, our successes; and the other people around us based on the foundation of how much money we are making, have and/or could be making. That's why we obsess about celebrities and materialism, because we assume that if you have money than you have everything.

As one whom has spent plenty of time in the company of those who "have it all," I can honestly tell you that is the furthest thing away from the truth. When you chase money, you seem to chase away everything else and sometimes that could even be your very own integrity. When you take a deeper look, you will see that many people who have wealth and are defined by it are completely unhappy and misunderstood. For many of these people, they have sacrificed so much of their true selves to obtain money that they don't even recognize who they have become and regret why they have become it. Most of these folks in the depths of their minds and darkest hours feel like; "yes, I got millions in the bank, but I have no real friends and no family to share it with, therefore, I am envious of you who is envious of me." You must understand that just like all other great things, riches and fame come at an even greater price. Furthermore, we don't really respect our own efforts or the efforts of others, unless there is a significant dollar attached to it. It is very true at least in American culture that the dollar leads every decision in our lives.

Based on the dollar; we decide what career paths we pursue, we decide who is fit to marry us, who are friends are, what schools we go to, what businesses we buy from, whether our efforts are working or not, what communities we live in, what churches we attend, what we give our time to as well as who we respect and who we don't respect. This is our greatest fault as human beings; we worship money and material items rather than people and experiences. Therefore, before we can dive into the exact reasoning behind desiring a different life, we must first be honest about the life we currently have and the choices that we have made to get there. Ask yourself, what do I desire most; money or happiness? Is my happiness dependent upon having money? Do I live life being lead by money? Do I examine people's worth by what they have rather than who they are?

For me, I realized that on the surface the answer to all of those questions was no. Simply because who wants to believe that they are that shallow or dare say that money is like God in their lives. Now, I could have stopped there because it didn't sound good to me that I would dare be like that. However, if I really wanted to solve my problems, I really had to revisit those questions and be truthful to myself. I, just like you didn't want to really know the truth, which was yes! By digging deep I realized that I was very guilty of all of those things as I was raised that way. Ok, now those who know me best know that I wasn't as deep into it as many others. I am a natural-born rebel, so many times I just go left because everybody else is going right, but I was still guilty nonetheless.

My mother didn't raise me to worship money, or use it as a value based measuring stick per se. However, society definitely did; especially, if you came into the world as a have-not. Those who have in life seem to the have-nots of life to always be happy. However, I realized that "seemed" was the key word, as the very naive ideal that those who have money are deliriously happy is the heavy burden of the wealthy. As I begin to gain success, I never really felt as successful as everyone else saw me to be. Especially from those who knew me from childhood, but I was expected to act like it. I was nowhere near financially wealthy but I was wealthy in social status and that seemed to greatly impress others.

The reasoning for my overall unsatisfied state as I searched deeply within; which you will also have to do; to grow and move on; was because I didn't feel like I was making as much money as my work deserved. On top of that I was putting it ahead of everything else. I felt extremely guilty about those factors and therefore I wasn't feeling as successful as I really was! I could not see what everyone else did as I was blinded by the hard work, the losses, the debts, the late nights, the many sacrifices, the let downs, and the loneliness that came with it. I was living my dream, but I wasn't happy because my bank account didn't reflect how far I truly came.

I beat the odds in every sense of the word, but because the money wasn't as great as the lifestyle of it all reflected, at some point I felt like I was on a treadmill to nowhere. Never mind the facts of everything that I overcame; such as beating the stereotypical ideals of being an urban African-American woman. According to American statistics: I should have become a drug addict, a stripper, oversexed, bitter, angry, dead, HIV infected, frequent trips to the county jail, and/or alone with more "baby-daddies" than I could count. However, none of these things reflected my life or me. Although, I do know some women experiencing some of that or coming from those backgrounds but the statistics do not reflect the majority of the African-American women that I know.

I never basked in the gratefulness of what I actually overcame. Such as the fact that as a 17-year-old, teenage mother, I actually made it through high school and graduated on time with no real guidance. Or, that I left my mother's house at 18 by getting on welfare and obtaining temporary rental assistance to working in corporate America. Or that I went to college obtained an associate's degree and decided to take a risk and not continue in exchange for pursuing my life long dreams. Or, that after suffering from a significant bout of depression, I became a local, self-taught radio and media personality, a second-generation photographer and a developer of five businesses. Or, that I was a good wife to a great guy that I was with for 20 years. Or, that I was a sensational mother of two great, socially and academically high-achieving kids. As well as through it all I became and was a well-respected and sought-after community advocate, media personality, entrepreneur, and had obtained many other great accomplishments along the way.

In the bigger scheme of things, none of this meant anything to me compared to having the money to do whatever I wanted. At that time that would have been the one and only thing that would have made me believe that I really made it! Made it where, you might ask? Out of the ghetto, the slums of America where the most talented people are born to rot and/or rise to unimaginable greatness. I still saw myself as not having enough, strained, lacking, and having something to prove but the reality was, that was the farthest thing away from the truth.

The realization of such truth is what began to change everything for me as I realized I wasn't living an unsatisfied life, but I was living with a false perception of my life that was making me unsatisfied! It was the false ideals of my own reality as I was psychologically defining my existence based on the conditions I was born into, my community's problems, and the struggles along the journey. So, no, I never could see myself like everybody else, because unbeknownst to me I was still seeing the old me and the stigmas attached to it. It didn't matter to me that I was completely different from the inside out that I had evolved gracefully. All I could see is the little, poor, misunderstood, mischievous and awkward urban black girl. A precocious child; living alongside a lot of her big although seemly impossible dreams.

I had to wake up and remind myself that although I was not financially wealthy, I was no longer under-privileged, either. My children were living a phenomenal lifestyle where they had everything they needed and more. The world was changing around me and needed my help more than ever. I was never hungry and I could obtain pretty much anything I desired. I was loved and respected by many and my life made a huge difference in the lives of others. God was always on my side as he never left me and I, with His instruction and mercy, accomplished dream after dream. I changed my perception, and in doing so like the ease and flick of a light switch it changed my reality.

Why should I change my reality?

Well, for one, since you are reading this book, it shows that you have some interest in changing the way things currently are in your life. On a deeper note, this is truly a question that only you can answer. You are the only one who really knows what's going on in your life and how you truly feel about it. So, let's stop right here for now and ask yourself; "Why should I change my reality?" For me, personally, there were many reasons why I wanted mines to change. Such as, the fact that I learned that I didn't desire success; I desired freedom!

The freedom that would give me the time that I wanted to become a better woman; a better human being; a healthier individual; more connected with God; making dinner at least five times out of the week; the time to read books, workout, bake, and to be adventurous. The Freedom that would allow me to walk away from the violence in my community and to joyfully spend more time with my family and friends. More importantly, I wanted the freedom to be more aware, true, and dedicated to fulfilling my purpose within the world. You must understand that you cannot let the comfort of being good rob you from the possibilities of being great!

Many of us are living accidentally, with lives that we are secretly unhappy with. Constantly wishing things were better, living from check to check, not evolving, wanting more, pretending things are great, postponing our dreams, perpetuating the rat race, overwhelmed with distractions, keeping up with appearances, overcompensating, living in the shadows of our reputation, and/or simply settling for less. However, if we all understood the very simple truth that we can and, for better or worse, currently are the creators of our own realities, then we could tap into the necessary power within to

9

change our current and future circumstances.

Although, change won't happen, unless you welcome, desire and/or allow it. Change is a great part of life and most concur that things change all the time, but what most don't realize is that change never happens by default. You have to participate either actively or inactively for change to take place; either way you can't be in a place of resistance. You should change your life, if you are unsatisfied with it and/or unsatisfied with yourself. If you are feeling like you rather spend your days and time doing this and that or being with these type of people or that person than a change is needed. Never underestimate the change a decision or a day can bring.

You cannot consider or continue living your life simply for the benefits of others, especially if it's not God. By that I mean you can't say, "well, I am going to stay at this job because they need me," don't worry about it as they will find someone else; or, "I am going to stay married to him/her because they need me," sorry to break it to you but they too will find someone else. You have to honor your relationship with yourself and God more than all others. By this I mean that you were created with a divine purpose. Yes, you; no matter what the situation is currently or what it has been in the past, you must understand that the world has not finished growing, developing and evolving.

Believe it or not, the world needs you to play your part for better or worse. If you are not pursuing your purpose or living it, then you are failing God and yourself. This is where your dissatisfaction really lives and breathes. Your soul is calling you home to a place of understanding that you are greater than. The ignorance of this truth is the very reason why you are torn between what you know and how you feel. Remember, the mind learns, but the soul is what teaches.

Sometimes our mind is our greatest enemy because it relies solely on reason, logic, and experience in which to translate understanding. However, your feelings or intuition has the direct connect between your higher self and God. The pain, frustration, unhappiness, stress, or simply the constant feeling that something needs to change is your indicator that the time is now. The more challenging the experience the more detrimental it is to your wellbeing. You can't live the life you want by lying about the life you currently have. You have to listen within yourself and you have to take action. If you want people to respect you for who you are, than you have to first become absolutely clear about whom you are yourself.

Next, you have to appreciate or change dependent upon whether you like or dislike yourself. After that simply embrace yourself and be honest about whom you are to all others. If you are pretending to be someone else that is because you don't like yourself. Although many of us do, I, could not dare live a lifetime willingly walking around with a mask. This is a huge part of why the world is so screwed up. I use to try to change the world but then I realized it was not the world who needed to be changed; it was the people who need to change. Transform your life because you desire more from it, change your life because you want to be who you were designed to be. Change your life because you know that where you are now is not reflecting it. Be courageous enough to walk your very own unknown, but destined path.

Am I worthy of my reality changing?

In modern day society, we are not taught to truly love ourselves. We are taught to emulate others, to pretend we know whom we are and to act as such. I never understood that, and I never was with it. This is probably why I have gotten into so much trouble as a kid and still do as an adult. How can we be ourselves if the people we love are entrusted with, and respect, are always telling us to be like someone else? It starts at home, with mom and/or dad trying to recreate a better version of themselves. Or they cast you in the shadow of an older or younger sibling; which they wish you could be more like. Further reinforcement of this idiocrasy takes place on our TVs, magazines, computers, books, peers, schools, and overall social circles, where everybody is pretending to be somebody else.

Before you know it, we are all confused and disillusioned grown-ups, who are completely absentminded of who we truly are. While starving to figure it out, depressed and wishing things were different we then simultaneously perpetuate this terrible cycle in our very own homes with our children. We, forcefully spend years molding little ones to fit into the cast iron ideals of society. While we secretly die within our very own cast iron prisons. This is the foundation for mid-life crises, and if you are ok with that path, then keep doing exactly what you are doing. If you are not okay with it, then I encourage you to keep reading. You must understand that a man who sees himself through the eyes of others is a man who has no true vision of his own identity.

You have always had an idea in your head about who you really are, how you wanted your life to be and who you really wanted to be in it. Although, somewhere down the line you accepted whatever came and stopped seeking what you truly desired. Some of you, like me, have been pursuing it all your life, but got there and realized it's not all that it seemed to be. Others of you may have not even started at all, as you may have selected to read this book in the explorative manner that a child sneaks a cookie. However, the good news is it doesn't have to stay like that, if you don't want it to. Yes, you are worthy of your reality changing, so much so that the world is dependent upon it.

That idea or dream you have is not a great act of your imagination, it's more like a window into the possibilities of yourself. It's a clue, a vision of where you truly belong, who you really are, and the affect you could have on others. God bestows upon you visions masked as dreams, that are unique and specific to you; providing you something tangible to entrust your faith upon. It's as if God opens a window so that you can see your possibilities within it. He will reveal either your position in this thing we call life, or it will be the very thing that clearly leads you to it. Therefore, you must vigorously pursue it! If we can paint, then we must paint; if we can sing, then we must sing; if we can write, then we must write; and if we can speak, then we must speak.

You were born to be the person who your dreams are revealing to you, every moment in your life, including reading this book, is a part of getting you there. Does this mean it will be easy? Absolutely not, it will be the most challenging aspect of your life to date. However, it's promised. Although, you have to be willing to do your part just as God and even I by writing this book are doing ours. Kudos to you as reading this is definitely a great first step or great 150th step, but then what?

The rest is truly up to you, and although there will be some challenges that will be easier than others, there also will be some that will make you feel like you are dying. Every time you get to those points, which are actually breakthroughs be extremely grateful as it reveals just how much closer you are. Understand, that's exactly what will be and is needed to happen; you in your current state will have to die so that the best of you can finally begin living. This type of personal reform will take extreme amounts of courage. You have to want it more than anything else! You will never arise to who you could be, if you don't let go of who you currently are.

Since this is completely personal, it will be extremely daunting at times as no one is going to give you a guide on you. You have to do all the work in complete solitude, outside of the many blessings that God will provide as evidence along the way. Ok, don't start buckling up and cracking under pressure, as you must remember you were born for this. This is your commitment and your personal sacrifice to God, which reveals; "how bad do you really want it?" So, are you worthy, is yet another personal question that you must ask yourself.

Are you worth what it will take to have a life that you enjoy living every day? Are you worth a body that will carry you in good health throughout the test of time? Are you worth love that will fulfill your heart and desire for as long as you walk the earth? Are you worth a six-figure salary or a multimillion-dollar company? Are you worth having a beautiful family, white-picket fence, dog, kids, college, retirement, and travel? Are you worth having mutually beneficial relationships that help grow and challenge you? Are you worth God's individual personalized attention? These are all questions based upon your own desires that you must ask yourself. These answers, will keep you on track, remind you of your purpose and provide you with great amounts of strength. They will also motivate you through your hardest moments and more importantly will tell you how worthy you are to yourself. Show God your faith alongside your work, and He will show you His hand.

How would my reality changing affect others?

We are all interconnected, and there is rarely ever a moment when we are not being watched or seen by someone. Even the slums of life have those who desire to be like someone within them. Within today's pop culture, social media has made it even faster and easier to reach people than ever before. Through the evolution of social media, most of us, for better or worse, are always broadcasting our lives or something that we have been touched by within them. Yes, we all know that your friends love to see your new haircut, your clients love supporting your new services, your family loves the pictures of the new baby and your haters/competitors love trolling your page looking for new reasons to hate you.

However, what many of us don't know is that we are really influencing others by our individual choices, actions, interest, likes, dislikes, purchases, thoughts, feeling and/or desires. These days we are all literally a part of the media. As individuals we are persuading each others thoughts and ideas simply based upon broadcasting our own! We are making a conscious or unconscious contribution to society via every post, comment, friend, follow, subscribe, share, like, tweet, add or delete.

A direct example of the power of this influence can be seen through how my life and work inspired a family in Cameroon to name their second-born daughter after me. The father asked for my blessing by telling me that it is customary for a child's namesake to be adopted from a person or thing that embodies the spirit of one whom the parents wish for the child to adopt. He said he wanted his daughter to become an asset to the world, as he felt that I was. Talk about being blown away and feeling unworthy although wise enough to know that this was no accident. I became even more empowered after this and she will soon be four years old and it is my desire to visit her before she turns six. As you can see, we all motivate, inspire, irritate, frustrate, support, appreciate, admire, celebrate, and change the people we come in contact with daily. We do this simply by living our very own lives because we are all interconnected. Everyone makes a contribution to the world and no matter how great or small what affects one affects all. The only question about this is; whether it's positive or negative effect.

If you are doing better in your life, you will treat others better and you will attract others who are also doing better. So, if I am happy and enjoying my life, and then I come in contact with you who are also happy and enjoying your life, and then we come in contact with others whom are also happy and enjoying their lives, then we have enough momentum to change the energy of any room, place and/or community at large. Think of all the miserable people, places, and things that you see around you daily, as most likely the people who you are currently in contact with are probably much like you are now; yawning for more.

That means they too are unsatisfied with their lives, they too want more, they too don't know where to begin. So, imagine what life would be like if we all started to change our realities for ones that are more favorable to each of us? Happy people are less likely to kill, steal, rob, hurt, rape, cheat, give you attitude, and any other horrible act that you can think of. Just like happy countries are less likely to go to war, throw bombs and kill their own people. I understand that for some of you, it will be difficult to look at yourself in this manner compared to the rest of the world or society. As it can definitely feel like you are so small that you don't even matter to the rest of the world, let alone are capable of changing it.

Based upon this, most people think what difference can I possibly make? However, if you are willing to try to understand the information I just gave you, you will clearly see that you could make all the difference in the world. At the very least you can make a difference to and for the people around you. You will inspire them, they will look up to you, and they will change themselves. Not because you set out to be the next Martin Luther King or Gandhi, unless that's what you want but because you empowered them by showing them what is possible. When you are being the best you, you motivate others around you to be the best them. Most of our own personal issues, just as the world's most daunting problems have the most simplistic answers. It's just because they are so simple that most don't believe in them; let alone ever give them a try.

For the world to be in its current condition, which is not so great, but then again, it is an absolutely great time to be alive, reveals how contrast leads us to places that we would not normally get to without it. Overall we are in environmentally, economically, socially, spiritually, and psychologically transformational times. Children are killing children all over the world, economies are collapsing, civil wars are breaking out and the ozone layer is melting. While at the same time a new age is emerging amongst the earth and people are becoming more involved in their local communities; children are walking us into a more blended future, absent of racism and intolerance; people are searching for ways to live better; they are challenging the status quo; corporations are losing control; people are writing and reading books like this in addition to so much more.

So, as the old saying goes, it always gets worse before it gets better, and that's because people are motivated more by pain and discomfort than love and wellbeing. With your help via your own personal development, it is very much possible that the world could evolve at a much faster, healthier, and peaceful rate. Therefore, why not be the one who kicks it off in your own life? You must understand that if a small number of people like yourself, who in a small number of situations, make a small number of different choices in a small number of circumstances those differences would grow into a large number of people who in a large number of situations make a large number of different choices in a large number of circumstances. You must believe that you are the very difference that the world needs now.

CHAPTER TWO

DEFINE A DIFFERENT REALITY

"I don't feel that you have to be in one particular box as you should dream big, think big, and accomplish big. It's simple as you are a combination of your thoughts, words, and deeds."

Keisha Knight Pulliam, Award Winning Actress

Now that I was finally clear on how far I truly came, what was holding me back, why I needed to change, and the power I truly possessed. My next step was to visualize exactly what my ideal life looked like. At this time, just like many of you, I was absolutely clear on what I didn't want, but unclear on what I did want. That was the easy part, as most of us spend our entire lives based upon what we don't want. When we are asked what we do want the mind draws a blank. The passion desists; the vigor is no longer apparent; the face releases its scrunched-up-wrinkles-in-the-forehead disposition and becomes more like you just took a muscle relaxer. Your mouth drops, jaws sag, and you find yourself wearing this face that screams clueless. Again, blame it on society as we are all viciously motivated by pain and discomfort. I, just as you, have made plenty or most of my decisions on the foundations of what I didn't want and never based off what I did want.

Growing up for me wasn't extremely hard, but it wasn't easy either. My mother and father split up when I was around three years old. My big sister of four years, Isis, was daddy's little girl and she took the separation pretty hard. Growing up for her was extremely difficult, as her life up until that point was full of stability. Isis experienced my mom in her best-self mode very similar to how I am now with my own children. I have two older brothers, Marcus who is deceased, and Roy, who is four years older than Isis. Marcus died at the age of 14, as he had a horrible elevator accident that involved some level of miscommunication between my father, Ronnell, and my mother, Dorothy that ultimately took his life.

I would imagine, that the death of Marcus left Roy, at 10 years old, feeling very alone and vulnerable. Although, he was still expected by society to go to school and perform as normal, which proved to be very difficult for him. Now with that being said, all these changes outside of the actual separation of my parents happened before my birth. While I was in my mother's womb, she was very distraught and angry; the life she knew, planned, and was living began to unravel in the most horrible ways possible. So when I was born, I came into the world kicking and screaming, a natural-born firestarter as my mom recalls it. Ready for anybody and anything! I never got to experience the joys that Isis did, so growing up we totally misunderstood the other. We were very much like two extreme forces who were exactly the same, but so very different.

As the old saying goes, hurt people hurt others, so to say the least, growing up we were more like strangers than sisters. Upon adulthood, we finally got it together, and she is truly my rock these days, and I love her more than words can ever express. Although, in the past it did sadden me when I thought about how we both missed out on each other's love for all of those years. However, we both continue to make up for it now as we supportively design our futures together. Minister Isis is the one person in my life who I know without a doubt will go to hell and back for me without even blinking an eye. She is an overall amazing woman and I am beyond blessed in this lifetime to have her as a sister and my truest friend. In between the death of Marcus and the birth of my younger sister, Marla, who is three years younger than me, I am assuming that the life of good times with both mom and dad were over. No more family trips to theme parks, picnics, and the many photoshoots by my father, as he too was a professional photographer as well.

Life for my family was never the same after my brother's death and the controversy that came with it as the relationship between mom and dad was getting worse and worse. It seemed that a piece of my mother died with her beloved son. It seemed that my father had to burden some of the blame for his death. It also seemed that neither one of them ever really got over it. I say seemed because I really don't know; this is just what I think based off the little I do. As I reflect upon my life, you must remember, this is in the womb and toddler time for me. Although what I do know is that my mother really pushed through it all. Even as a young child, I was always aware of and very sensitive to my mother's pain. Throughout my childhood I could clearly see and feel her hurt.

Now, I never felt like I lacked the great life of my family because I didn't remember those times and I never lacked love. So, unlike Roy and Isis, I never yearned for that life because truthfully to me, I never experienced it. Growing up, my brother Roy seemed to always be fine. I say this because Isis took it really hard and now having children of my own I can clearly understand why. Roy had a mild temperament, which I am sure it was because as a male, he was raised not to be sobbing and distraught. He was different from the other guys in the community, as he was a mama's boy.

I love my big brother; he used to cook for us and even do our hair while maintaining his masculinity, of course and he's a chef at this very day. I only knew my mom as she was then and my father was out of the picture at this point; so I really didn't know him at all. Because of this as a small child, I quickly created a defense mechanism that still sticks with me today. I learned to accept the things that I could not change and to change the things that I could. I told myself that it is in my best interest to just let it go. Growing up my mom seemed to be emotionally distraught and secretly very unhappy, due to the death of her eldest son. It seemed to some degree she became numb to the emotions of her children; present but numb.

As life continued to evolve, my mother met my stepfather Antoine. Together, they had my youngest two siblings, Antoinette and Mark, who are five and eight years younger than me. Now for my mother, that is a total of seven children and I was her middle child. Things were financially and emotionally hard. We learned early on that we only had one another and that we had to support and take care of each other. My stepfather, Antoine, who just recently passed away a few months ago from the time of this writing, was a great man and a Haitian immigrant. I truly respected and loved him, as I know he did me. He was the only example of a father outside of Bill Cosby and my friend's dad Mr. Henry Austin that I knew. He was always kind to me and my siblings, but my mother limited how close he could actually be with us because of her own past experiences. More importantly, to make sure that her girls, which she had four, were protected and never violated by a man whom we were supposed to trust.

So, with all that being said, I stepped up at a very early age. As far back as nine years old, I remember being very hands-on with my little sisters and brother. When my mother was gone, I took it upon myself to be mommy. As I grew, I quickly became a go-getter aka a hustler, so I would go to the store for people, bag at the local supermarket, make and sell key chains and pens out of string some call it lanyard. I would take my proceeds, and buy sandwiches, popcorn, three-liter sodas, and ice cream for shakes. My little sisters, brother, and I would then have fake picnics in the house; watch movies, and create fun games with one another. Imagination was absolutely necessary back in those days – and we definitely used ours.

My mother Dorothy is my greatest hero, and I love her to death, as she did her absolute best for us. While growing up, we never went hungry, never had our lights, heat, or phone cut off, which others experienced often in our community. She too debunks the ideas of a stereotypical-urban, black woman. My mother never did drugs or alcohol and she never dated a lot of men or participated in any of the other wide spread lies about black women. My mother is and has always been an extremely hard working and giving woman. She always protected us and gave us all that she had to give. My mother is where I get my servant-for-the-people, attitude from. As early as I can remember, my mother worked at the Lincoln Motel as a housekeeper and desk clerk around the corner from where we lived.

This place was where the forgotten and broken were sent or came to live. So these were the druggies, throwaways, runaways, prostitutes, handicap, homeless, drug dealers, and simply people who were down on their luck. However, my mother never looked at these people any differently. She never judged them, and she never allowed them to influence her actions or behaviors. What she did do was love them, support them, feed them, listen to them, and always gave them an encouraging word. Even through her own pain, suffering, and not ever having enough, she truly loved those people and they loved her back

I clearly remember bringing food to them, going to the store for them, listening to their lives and how they got in the situations that they were in. I hopefully listened to their plans to rise out of their current circumstances, which some did and some did not. I was a very peculiar and curious child; I absolutely loved people. I was so fascinated by other people's lives. Truth be told, I still am and the stranger you are the more I want to know about you. I go places simply to excitedly people watch and wonder. I use to try to figure out why but at this point I don't think there is a need to explain it. It's my thing, my most significant interest as I am a people collector. It's just who I am.

As a kid, I loved to read but who needed books? I had real-life stories of real people who used to be rich and now were homeless; who had degrees, but drugs caused them to lose it all; pretty women who sold their bodies for milk to feed their babies; or artistic drug dealers who really didn't like what they were doing. These men felt like it was all they could do and it gave them a sense of power to feel like a real man. Providing an opportunity to be one of value to the people in their lives. Talk about contrast; these things amazed me and simultaneously, unbeknownst to me was training me in what not to do. It was a place where the faces constantly would change, but the stories always were the same.

As an active community servant myself, I am just realizing in this very moment as I write this that my mother probably needed them just as much as they needed her. They gave her a sense of worth greater than her own problems; greater than her own responsibilities and greater than her own heartache, pain and lack. They revealed the humanity within her. They respected and honored her as the Queen that she truly was. If there was no other place in the world that my mother could go, to be recognized fully for who she truly was and to feel like a "Somebody"; she could always go to the Lincoln Motel. No matter how little we had, my mother always showed and taught us that we always had something to give and to be grateful because the circumstances within our lives could always be worse.

With all of that being said, I grew up always desiring more and wanting to be better! I was always planning my life; right down to the smallest and most trivial of things. Such as "I'm always going to have juice in my house, I'm always going to keep paper towels, I'm not having a lot of kids and I'm not doing this or doing that!" However, the deeper truth was that my desires were being born from a place of resistance. Their foundation was based off of what I didn't want in my life based upon the life I was born into and the insight I was receiving from the people around me.

I became strong because of the weakness I had seen,

I became real because of the fakeness, I became a rebel because I didn't want to be normal, and I refused to give up on my dreams because so many others had. Growing up, many people thought I would be nothing or maybe they secretly wished I would just like many of them. You see, as a kid I was precocious and always was too sure of myself in the eyes of adults. They would look at me and speak to me as if they were asking; "who are you to be so convinced about who you are?" I would look at them and speak to them as if I was saying, "I am worthy and don't blame me because you don't think the same about you."

I became the great mother I am by way of all of the things my mother gave and couldn't give me. When I unexpectedly became pregnant as a teen, I made the decision that I could not fall any deeper into a stereotype than I already was. I was determined to finish school on time and make a positive example of myself. I was determined to prove everybody wrong who thought I would be nothing. I fell in love, got married and stuck it out through the most difficult times because of all the broken families in my community.

I truly wanted more for my children. In the moments when I felt like I could no longer bare my relationship, it was the overall conditions of the community that always saved my marriage. By that I mean as a radical activist at the time, and a black woman, I would do everything possible to fight for my family to be an example of the change that is so desperately needed to develop our communities from the inside out. All that sounds great, but then again, when you dig deep, you see that these desires all came from the outside of me based upon what I didn't want. None of them came from a place of what I did want.

Once I reflected upon all of those things, I realized that I could turn it all around. That in this very lifetime I could give myself a second chance by creating an opportunity full of possibilities based upon what I truly desired. I exchanged the rat race, which was the one society placed me in, for an ideal that I myself created. I developed this ideal, from a place of understanding and well-being, which unbeknownst to me was loosely always my life's motto and of course that ideal is Start Living Your Best Life Now. So, I thought about my best life in a very specific and laser-focused way.

What would happen in my ideal life from the time I awoke until the time I slept? What environment would I like to be in? What type of people would I like to see? What type of person would I be? How would I respond to my children? How would my children respond to me? What type of wife would I be? What type of husband would I have? What would I be doing with my time? What type of friends would I have? What type of family member would I be? The list went on and on. When I answered those questions, I thought what you are probably thinking right now; ok, great we are on our way as the hard part is done. No, that wasn't even the half of it, as I then realized that the real hard work was to make the decision if I was going to continue living the way I was, or if I was going to make the actual decision to start living my best life now.

What does my different reality look like?

You should know by now that I love asking personal questions. Let's take a moment, and think about this in the most holistic way possible. When I say holistic, I mean don't go into your dream of being a rock star and stop there. Dig deep and think about your family, your friends, your health, your children, your spirituality, and your affect on others. Imagine your life as the whole person you truly want to be, as it will take each of those elements cohesively working together to really have a full, happy, healthy, and productive life. This will take vigorous thought and extreme visualization, as you need to see, feel, and smell what is that you want. Anything less than that is just being good or having a particular high skill set in one area or another, which may or may not bring you complete fulfillment. As for each of you, your answers will be different.

Remember, there is no right or wrong answer, you are not being tested, no grade to acquire, no one is going to question why you want that and/or try to change your mind. This is all about and between you and your life! Take a few moments or days and ask yourself this; what does my ideal life look like? Jot your thoughts down on something, so you can come back to them when you need a reminder. Don't think about what can't be and why it wouldn't work or what your current situation is. Just simply and freely think about what you truly want and desire. You really can have it all so don't let one of your dreams or fears be the robber of the rest of your life.

So many of us are doing so little in our lives that when we see anybody doing just a little bit of something, we are looking up to them like they are Jesus. All the celebrities on TV or in your local community, you watch them star struck as if they are pulling people out of burning buildings or teaching young minds every day. These are our real heroes and the people who quietly live a life that fully reflects who they are and what they desire. For example, in my ideal life, I don't desire riches and fame; although if it happens, it just happens. What I want is peace! I want to be able to get up at 5 or 6 a.m. every morning and get centered. This involves me praying, showing gratitude via praise, reading the Bible, meditating, stretching, and working out.

After that, I want to began making my contribution to the world by doing my daily work of reaching out to the people with an inspirational thought to get them started on their day; then create and share empowering resources, whether that be through a blog post, a coaching session, a webinar, a meeting, an interview, a conversation and/or a speaking engagement. Then, I want to have a nutritious lunch and make a very nutritious dinner for my family. After that, I want to be free to do whatever I want, whether that be hang out with friends, a business lunch and/or dinner, go-kart riding, yoga, trolling the bookstore, going to an event, pool, Zumba, movies, or whatever I desire. I just want to be able to do the work I believe that I was put on earth to do and make a good enough living so that I can contribute to my household and do the things I desire.

Simple enough, but when you are not trained to live in such a manner, it becomes a transformation rather than just a few mundane actions. As you see, I am not asking for much, skipped a few details, but that's the gist of it overall. I lived a fast enough life to know that I enjoy the simple things, which always leads to the extraordinary things. So, as I currently write this, I am still not getting up at 5 or 6 a.m. as these days that's more like bedtime, and my rise time is noon or 1 or later. I know, I know! Some of you wish you can stay in the bed until noon or later., but when you have done that and been there, you will notice you start wanting other things and over time those things will change. Others of you maybe like "I could never stay in bed that late," but either way it doesn't matter as you are living for you now and not by the measuring stick of what others do.

Yes, I too have more work to do when it comes to living my best life, but you will find out for yourself that it is an evolving practice based on a consistent decision to do so. As I mentioned before about my wanting to get up earlier, that's only because in my new career as a Life Coach and Motivational Speaker, I want to assist you in getting up, out, and excited about your day every morning. I am doing extremely well in the other areas of my life that I have challenged myself to implement, and I have a few more to work on but it's all in due progress as change takes time. For now, you cannot tell me that I am not Rachael Ray up in this kitchen! I make the best 30-minutes-or-less, healthy meals that you can think of, and I started a little baking. My DSLR and cell phone went from having mainly pictures of people on the red carpet to homemade banana nut bread and grilled chicken and asparagus with brown rice, lemon, and parmesan sauce; shots of me doing yoga; studying the Bible; and go-kart racing. I'm loving it!

To be very transparent and honest with you, there is only one area in my life that is going to take much more time than the others to implement, because it involves exit and acquirement strategies. By this I mean, there are going to be some things in your life that you want to change, but you have to be strategic about them, like quitting your job, changing majors, getting a divorce, or waiting until your kids grow up. So be patient, but be diligent! My personal goals of peace and simplicity may not sound like much to you, but trust, for me, it's the best thing ever. So again, it's all about you and what you really want now. Life is too great to live in the shadows of the ideals of others!

What type of commitment will I have to make for my

new reality?

Ok, so now that you have done all that thinking and visualizing you have to now make a decision and it's the same decision that I too had to make. Do you dump your current reality for this proposed new one, or do you close this book now and keep living your mundane life? Full of, I could have done that, I was going to do this but, I wish I could have done that, some day I'm going to, etc., etc., etc., or more like blah, blah, blah. You don't even believe it when you are saying it. Oh, did I offend you? Well, hey, let's be honest, you know your life is mundane by your own standards or you wouldn't be reading this book. This book is for people who are determined, for the desperate, for the courageous, for the dreamers, for those who have nothing to lose, for those who want it, for those who could no longer ignore the voice inside of them, for those dying for a change, for those who are willing to try anything and for those who are wishing things were differently!

The people who read this book are about to do one out of two things. They are either about to make it happen in their lives, because they know that all the things that have ever happened to them up until this moment were preparing them for this moment in time. They know that they are worthy, that they are capable, that they are committed, that they can do it, and that they must do it. Or, they will be the ones who will call it quits and bury themselves consciously in a life full of regret. They will be too afraid, they will feel like it's impossible, they will believe that they are too deep into their current situation to ever get out, and ultimately they will lack the courage needed to face their own selves. A man who fears his own shadow is a man who fears the world.

Ok, you've decided to keep reading, so that makes me

believe that you have made the commitment to leave your old reality for your new one or at least you are strongly considering it! I am very happy for you, as you have made the right decision. Based on my story alone, you will see how even the best of us could get caught up and sidetracked. Or, rather your experiences could push you onto a path that you never really signed up for. Life is full of making life-altering decisions without having all the facts to make the most effective choice for the long term when you made them. So, why the hell do you have to become imprisoned by them? I've found that you don't and that's the good part!

Now for the bad news, the path to living your best life, although rewarding, will not be easy. It will definitely be one of the hardest challenges in your lifetime. Transforming your life does not come easy, simply because your life does not involve just you. As well as the fact that it is a personal journey. You are the judge and jury, you set the laws and you have to discipline yourself. You will have to be courageous and vulnerable at the same time. Now, if you are starting out pretty early in the game, and you have no children and are not married, then, it will be a little easier as that removes a few obstacles, but it will not be a breeze.

The reason for this is because we are used to others telling us what to do, when to do it, and how to do it. Also when you choose to transform your life, there are no others. It's just you. You purge the junk, the bias, the hate within, you set the goals, you determine what is good enough and what is not. You set the challenges, you record the progress, you design and follow the exit strategies, and you are literally alone within it. No one will wake you up and say, go to the gym; no one will say, don't eat that; no one will say, take that client, don't take that one; no one will say, go here or go there, and no one will tell you to do this or do that. It's just you, your higher-self, and God. Sometimes, it's a good thing for a man to be an island all by himself.

The ultimate commitment that you will be making is to stop living by default and to start living on purpose. You will be an active participant in the fulfillment of your destiny, the writer of your book, and the president of the land of you. It will be difficult at times, but it will be rewarding always. For the first time in your life, you will see what you are really made of and you will be the master of your own actions and thoughts; constantly consciously choosing. You will see what your true skills are, what your character really is, and you will exuberate a certain level of confidence that will be unmatched. You will know that you are the one. The one who is greater than, the one who deserves all that you have ever dreamed, the one who will go to the ends of the earth to show themselves what they are truly made of.

You will see that your life will begin to change as your ideas, thoughts, understanding, and awareness sharpens. You will see and hear things that others can't, and it won't matter to you if they don't see it as you will feel blessed that you did. Your experiences will be very fulfilling as they are the ones you choose. Yes, you still will have days where you don't feel so great, because the challenge in itself seems too much to bare, but you will feel it and acknowledge it. Then the next day or a few days later you will be right back up on your horse simply because it feels better and you have the power to choose. If one is ever given the option to choose, one should never choose to lose.

How do others see and respond to me in this new reality?

Others will see a difference within you, too and they will begin to shift their behaviors around you. You will see that your energy will shift rooms, halls, places, and circumstances, as you will be the one who makes all the difference. There will be some who will be very welcoming of this as they are attracted by that type of energy, and they will start to ask you what are you doing or what are you on because they could definitely use some of that in their lives. Then, there will be others who will not like it, as they want you to go back to being the old you for their own purposes. As they can't use the new you as the new you is too sure about what you want and what you feel and the best ways for you to be productive. However, you don't have to worry about them as you will not be able to tolerate people, places, and/or things that do not reflect your interest or that you know are beneath you and it's an also a requirement.

There will be a lot of detoxifying, which we will get into further in the next chapter. However, on a greater note; people will see and respond to you as you intend for them to do so. Remember this is not a situation where you walk into a room and anything just happens, this is more like you walk into a room and the room adjusts to you. So, if you are happy, excited, and full of life, your energy will transform that space at least while you are in it. If you feel that there is a greater energy in the room, that is the complete opposite of yours, than that's a room you get the hell out of. It is always better to be one who gets a greater use of self than anyone else.

Life is truly about energy, and I have been using the power of energy my entire life so much so that when people meet or converse with me whether in person, over the phone and/or via the computer, they often say I love your energy. Now, that's such a simple statement, but energy is not a mainstream term. It's more or less used by people who are on a spiritual level, or for those dream-catchers. Meaning, people who have a higher awareness of life in general. However, this term has been widely used by children, politicians, celebrities, the uneducated, the educated, gangsters, the so-called low lifers and all types of random folks to express appreciation about or to me.

I'm even sure that by now you can feel my energy, you pretty much know whom I am, and you know that you can trust me. It's not just because of the words on these pages, as they go directly to your mind. It's because you can feel my spirit talking to your spirit and it's the very reason why you keep reading. That's a beautiful human connection; don't you think? The experience that we are currently sharing in this very moment as writer and reader is valuable evidence regarding the power of energy. So for better or worse, we all are always transmitting energy to one another. That's why you can go in a place and be completely cool, and then come out and be drained, angry, or hungry. Emotions are just that, fluid energy in motion.

You know those moments in life; when you felt like I was ok until I went into that store, and then I started to feel sick, or I was feeling good until I talked to so and so? Yes, those moments. This happens because unbeknownst to you the energy of someone else was transferred over to you, and maybe the store you went into someone was sick at work, or in the owner's family, or when you talked with such and such, you hung up and took their pain with you. So just like the negative can jump on you, so can the positive and it goes either way as energy can bounce on or off of you. The more conscious you are of it, the more power you have to reject and accept other people's energy as well as to release or withhold your own.

Although, energy is always in motion, so you can't really store it and that's why it's always changing. However, you can build on yours so that it could be so strong that it is hard for others to get through it. Life is full of Alphas and it will always be someone who is stronger and/or better; I guess that is God's way of keeping us humble. Therefore, it is extremely important as you change your reality to harness the power of your own energy. This will be the key to guiding you on your path. Your feelings will be transmitted through your energy, and if your feelings are not good than your energy is not good. If your energy is not good than your experiences and the others who come around you will reflect that not feeling good energy, and vice versa. You must remember that you were born to be the sun of your very own universe.

CHAPTER THREE

DETOX YOUR CURRENT REALITY

"The world on a greater scale is bigger than that, it's hard but it takes the small things to make the big changes. If there is a will, then there is a way. It takes sacrifice and you've got to go through it to get to it."

Black Thought of The Roots, Hip Hop Artist

Once I made the decision to stop living by default and to start living on purpose, I, like you probably are right now, was feeling really good about myself. I felt like I was finally going to be able to take full control of my own life; from a position of freedom rather than from a position of bondage. I was jumping out of the rat race, I didn't need to watch the numbers, I wasn't trying to convince anyone of my worth and value! I hated selling anyway, as I am more of an informer-type person. Although, I realized I was selling people all the time. Trying to convince them on why they should do this or that. Very much like how organized religion tries to sell you on God with fear.

You know the mantras; if you don't do this, God is going to do that, or you won't have everlasting life. Why not just let you know how much God loves you? Why can't they just tell you, that He has your back no matter what, as He created it; that you don't have to be perfect, because He already knows that you are not, and He loves you anyway. You can show God your love in return by doing what He created you to do. It's really that simple because He needs you to. Have you ever considered the possibility that God needs you to partner with him? Have you ever considered that it is through us that God does his greatest work?

When you understand that about God, you obtain a certain level of peace in your spirit that all things will be well and will turn out for the best. Even if it takes a few trips back and forth to hell to get there, at the end, you will see that everything that happens in your life for better or worse are always in your best interest. Your experiences are like compasses guiding you as you evolve into who you were meant to be. The experiences and the ups and downs within them never cease. They are the totality and the reflection of the evolution of you; never fully complete and are always a work in progress. So in reality, your problems are actually your opportunities and the worse the circumstance the greater the possibilities are to grow.

The issue here is that most of you believe the opposite, when you are faced with adversity; you began to shrink. You waste time asking why me, and then you get stuck in the haze. You allow your fears to take control and you begin to abandon your faith. What you need to do is not ask why but what next? You need to begin looking at your issues as areas in your life that need to improve. Fear is a natural and humbling emotion that we all experience it but to face it you must tap into your courage. For you to exhibit courage you must move beyond your fears. This gives you the ability to take action and push past the isolated stillness that fear traps you in. So welcome your fear as an opportunity to be courageous.

Because of fear as human beings, we find the need to want to control everything and this was a huge issue for me. I never saw myself as fearful but I had to be a fearful person because I really didn't trust others or God for that matter with my overall wellbeing. In my mind, I am self-made, and the things I overcame and learned were independent of direct human instruction. So like you, maybe, I thought I knew it all. I learned early on, that if I wanted something for myself, it was up to me to go get it or most likely it would never happen.

Therefore, I would jump all in with everything I had, and I would stop at nothing until I obtained it. By this, I mean by my need to control the outcome, I left no space for others to help me or more importantly for God to do His part. Yes, faith without work is definitely dead, but work without faith is simply stupid. I knew that everything I ever did and accomplished in my life was because I always had a sixth sense that God was with me. He was constantly instructing me to take this or that action outside of my mischievousness, but the way in which I went about those actions were totally from a place of free will.

I didn't realize that my fears blocked my ability to trust. I was so fearful that someone would get it wrong, let me down or didn't care that I would just do it myself or go without it. I thought that I was having faith in God, but the truth was I was having faith in me and that's why I needed to be so involved. I was so afraid that I was trying to control the outcomes of everything. I learned this truth about myself in a devastating and heart-wrenching way. Which was the actual birth of the need to take action now against that wrestling feeling inside of me; the one that was alarming me that things in my life seriously needed to change. This is what ultimately propelled me onto this path.

This particular circumstance happened four years ago and involved me randomly meeting someone and falling madly in love with them, although I was married with children. The guilt of such truth and the pain it caused as well as not being able to fully experience such love devastated me. See, I never imagined that two people could fall in love in a minute of meeting one another and love each other so deeply but never be together. Yes, I read it in stories, watched it in the movies, but I have always believed and still do in the power of love and its ability to overcome all. Silly me, as I am a hopeless romantic and I believe there is no such thing as impossible.

In addition I thought I already met and married the man whom I would be with forever. By way of this "next lifetime" experience and all that came with it my soul became awakened. Or rather the outside version of myself finally caught up with the inside version. At that time, I could not understand what was happening to me. How could I become so captivated by someone to the point that I no longer recognized myself? Throughout the years to follow, due to the fact that I am both hardheaded and insightfully gifted; for God's purposes I needed to be completely broken down.

I could not depend solely on my mind to gain understanding of how I ended up in such an unfamiliar place. My mind as it pondered began to stretch itself to the limits because of the pain, stress, confusion, frustration, and turmoil behind this situation. So much so that it began to tell me that something was wrong with me, and that I must be delusional. I eventually learned that I could not change or ignore the circumstances, and it challenged me to unwillingly change myself. God always has your back, and even like human parents, some time, He has to teach you in a not-so-feel-good way, so that you can get back up on your path, or so you can make a left, right, or U-turn.

It's funny how when you are desperate you start to really search for God's voice. You start to let your tiny brain take a vacation. This is because the mind is a powerful tool, but as stated in chapter one, the mind is limited and can become our greatest enemy as it only has logic and experience to rely on. Therefore if a situation or experience has never happened to you before and you don't know anyone else it's ever happened to and if you can't understand why it's happening then you start to think you are out of your mind and basically crazy. However, the truth is sometimes in order for God to get your attention you do need to be out of your mind. As God wants you to know that the answer is not there; the answer is with him, and He is trying to get your immediate attention.

Those who recognize this at some point come out of their tragedies while those who don't, stay trapped within them and for some, they perish simply because they can't take it. Through my ongoing tragic experience I just expressed, God has showed me, who I really am and how I needed to abandon my theory of being alone; as I am never alone. He has always been with me, although I have not always been with him. He taught me that I could not depend on others for the things that I could only obtain through Him. God also revealed to me a higher level of consciousness within, which is the actual link between the instant love I experienced and myself.

All of this and my actions within it made me realize that in many ways my desire and passion to help others was causing me to be a huge blessing-blocker. My go-getter spirit was pushing the things I desired the most away from me. The blessing-blocker aspect was based on the fact that people were dependent upon me in my life, which essentially was everyone. I was basically everything to everybody. I was your friend, your teacher, your mentor, and your living Jesus. Who needed God in their life when they had me? No matter what your problem and/or issue, I always had an answer, a blueprint, or an idea to get you over, under and/or around it. No need to pray, just call Real, she will figure it out for you.

If I were born in Africa, I would probably have been an oracle. People would have journeyed high and low to my village with some kind of offering and in exchange, I would give them the answers to their most daunting questions. I am like an emergency-management type of person as the big things in life are always easy for me to figure out, and the simple things are the things that get under my skin. So, I could tell you what to do to get your life on the right track, but I probably wouldn't be the best person to tell you what bus to take to get where. Then on the go-getter tip for myself, as stated earlier, I would be so involved and unbeknownst to me, at the time, non-trusting that I did not provide the space for others to do their part or for God to conduct His miracles.

This lead me to always feel alone; I always felt like people dealt with me like I was superwoman rather than another human being with needs too. I never had mutually beneficial relationships; I had to do everything myself; I was very impatient, felt unsupported, very aggressive as a woman; although still loving and feminine and I had an all-or-nothing attitude. Therefore I wasn't getting what I desperately needed from the people in my life; no guidance, no nourishment, no protection and no real support. I never knew when to quit as being a quitter or rather letting something go was never really an option for me; especially if I did not accomplish what I was trying to obtain.

In order to transform my life I had to first sift through and acknowledge what the self-sabotaging patterns were and let them go. This was because I had to accept the reality that my life for better or worse was all my doing. I had no one to blame, as I was mainly living based of off my reactions to the limitations society had set forth and my perception of it all. Therefore my experiences and the people in my life were reflective of that. Basically, I, just like many of you, led my life as a victim who was just fighting back. I realized that I actually wasn't living life at all; I was simply responding to it. The first half of my life, which most likely has been and/or is the same as yours, can be likened to being in a hospital and fighting to survive.

Your state of wellbeing is based off of just being there and coming out of what you have just been through. So, yes, I was good at surviving, but I wanted to be great at thriving. I didn't want to live my life like that anymore. I went from someone who wanted to be to someone who did and then the time in my life had came for me to be someone who is. To move forward you must be clear on what held you up in the first place to be able to truly go beyond it or you are doomed to repeat it.

You might be asking what is that? Well, it's when you are not caught up in the hype, when you have been there, done that, and you are clear on what and who is really important to you and why. When you are extremely dedicated to realizing and being no less than who you were designed to be even if that means you have to walk away from everything you have ever known because it stands in the way. When you have nothing to prove, when you are not willing to superficially sell your soul for things to look like something for people you care and don't care about. When you can let things go and as well as live and love unconditionally.

When you can clearly see things for what they are, and when you have the courage to truly face yourself and others for who they are. When you are willing to keep moving progressively forward by your own standards. When I speak of moving forward, I mean to keep learning, experiencing, searching for answers, and taking chances. You must understand that life is not simply limited to making a living, having a family, and waiting to die. It's about clearly seeing that the world doesn't just have an affect on you, but you have an affect on the world and therefore you need to be living your best life within it.

Do I have to remove things from my current life for my new reality?

Yes, you do! When you are determining who, what, and how to give your energy, time, insight, and love you must understand that everything matters even in the smallest detail. You have to let go of the fantasies and face the realities; only the raw truth will do. As nothing just happens, and life is too important to be ruled by the untruthful, the persuasive ego and the crippling feelings of both hate and fear. You will absolutely have to give these sidekicks up, as they are best life now blockers. Ego, hate, and fear are very dangerous factors in life. The ego is too concerned with the image part of a being, hate is too concerned with the ideals and actions of others, and fear is too concerned with limitations.

I have always been a martyr of the truth, as it has always been my measuring stick and my greatest way of expressing my love. Now many whom have been slashed by my stick of truth would say, love is probably the last thing they felt while receiving it. For better or worse I have always told and stated the truth out of sincere love. I love people so much so that I rather would tell them the truth for their own personal growth and have them leave me than to lie for my own comfort and have them stay with me. As I know at some point, they will get it and respect me for it, and if not, then that's ok, too, but at least I did my part in the eyes of God.

The ego stops people from being truthful, because the ego wants to be the king or queen of everything. So you can like them or hate them simply because they are so much better and that's where ego stores its esteem. Those who are lead by ego can't be truthful about themselves and others as it sacrifices not being liked or reveals a less-than perspective. The ego is more concerned with being right than anything else. Hate also stops people from being truthful, because it wants to dislike so badly that often times an enemy of the one you hate becomes your friend simply because of the mutual hatred you have between you.

Therefore, those who are lead by hate despise the truth, as it may debunk the reason why they are hating in the first place. By this I mean, hate will deny the truth because by accepting it as such, it then takes away the very reasoning proposed to hate. Fear is the worst emotion and most dangerous dynamic known to man, as fear is a crippler. It does not care about the truth, it is just there to stop you from doing anything because you fear x, y, and z. So those who are led by fear are in the worst place possible because the truth for better or worse is the last thing they want to deal with. Fear just goes on pretending things are ok and blaming others for everything. Stop hiding behind your fears and playing the daunting blame game. Start taking responsibility for your own life!

Yes, it's true you had a little help, but ultimately for better or worse you got your own self wherever you currently are. Remember the you, that people know or think they know is the you that you have shown to them. By now, you should definitely see that of course you are going to have to let go of many things from your old reality to live your new one. Especially those self-destructive patterns I spoke about earlier. Think about it, how are you going to transform something old into something new without adding, subtracting, multiplying, and dividing a few things?

Consider Play-Doh, and how much fun you used to have with it as a kid. You would take a blob of it, and make something interesting, love it, then squish it into another blob, and create something else. You start ripping it in half, and then taking other colors and mixing them in. You would get whatever will stick to it, and make eyes, noses, or whatever you want, but before you knew it you have created something else. You either loved what you had created so much so that you let it harden, and you kept it. Other times you would squish it up again and start over, or just put it up in its container until next time.

This is the same process that you must constantly do in your life as many times as it takes, until it fits great. When it is no longer great then it's time to repeat the process, as this is the everlasting cycle of life. The sooner you accept that is the sooner you will begin to appreciate and navigate through life better. There are no lifetime-forever guarantees that I or anyone can offer you as you must understand the more you live and the more you experience is the equivalent to the more you grow and evolve. Life is a progressive process of constant movement through gradual stages.

When you stop evolving, that's when you need to be seriously worried, as who you were yesterday should not be the same as who you are today. Many of you feel this way now and this is why you wish things were differently. You feel that the people, places, and things that worked in the past are no longer working in your present and you feel guilty about it. Nothing is wrong with those feelings because its your indicator that its time to go to the next level. Understand that, you don't expect to wear the same shoe size forever, or, for your toothbrush to last you a lifetime, so don't think the people, places, things, and ideals in your life are supposed to give you such guarantees.

That's where we go wrong as we are lead by ego, hate, and fear, as all three of those dynamics have convinced you that what you said, liked and did yesterday must be the same for all of your days. They say it is because it shows commitment, credibility, and consistency. Whoever said that should be stoned to death! All it reveals and perpetuates is limitation based on the superficial. Locking yourself in a prison of your very own making is the most ridiculous thing that a person can willingly submit to. The sad part is that most of you have forgotten that change is to evolution what not breathing is to death. Most of us say that there is no guide to life but it truly is and it specific to each of us; it's called intuition.

As you live your life, you are constantly receiving new pieces of information daily, and this info should be expanding you as a whole person. To allow the natural process of evolution, you cannot be tightly bounded to the thoughts and ways of the past you. You also have to consciously be selective about what you are actually allowing within. By this I mean, if you think and feel differently; why are you getting up everyday acting like you don't think and feel differently? Why are you engaging with and exposing yourself to the people, places and things you don't want while shutting yourself off to the things that you do desire?

"I don't want to be a criminal, but everything I do is about being a criminal; I don't want to be with him or her, but everything I do, I am still doing it with him/her; I hate my job, but every morning I keep going to it; I really want a dog, but I keep taking care of this cat; I don't really like living here, but I keep paying the rent month after month; I really do love this person, but I never show them; I love this car or house, but I really can't afford it; I don't think he or she is my friend or that I can trust them, but I keep spending all my time with them; or I know that I really love her or him, but I keep staying with this one or that one;" and the list goes on and on.

If any of this, sounds like you or anything else similar that was not mentioned, then it just proves my point further. Ask yourself; why am I participating in the BS? Can you see that you are being lead by ego, hate, or fear? Hopefully you can, because you are but the good news is you don't have to keep doing so. However, you must give up your superficial ideas about living and life.

Your ego won't let you call it quits because the job pays a lot, the chick is hot, the car makes you look cool. It tells you that you can't risk everything you've worked for simply to be happy, as that's stupid. The hate, whether it's self-inflicted or outward, won't let you let go. It tells you that because someone hurt you in the past that all men and women can't ever be trusted. It tells you that you can't ever be or do anything else, as the world set you up for failure. That everyone is against you so its ok for you to be mean, rude and mistrusting. The fear will never let you stop, because you are not worthy to be with that person. It tells you that you don't really want to know that about yourself, so you just keep closing your eyes to it, and lying to yourself. It tells you that it won't work out; so don't try. It asks you, who are you to want to quit your job? It tells you that you are too deep into your current circumstance, and could never turn back now. When you let go of the ego, the hate, and the fear, you simultaneously welcome in everything else.

What if they are people, places, and things that I love dearly?

For better or worse, when your life is evolving, as most of our lives are, you are constantly making commitments and bringing more and more people, places, and things within it. Most don't realize that each of these factors is extremely important, as they dictate the overall direction and theme of our lives. I don't care who you think you are; look at your friends and you will really see who you are; look at your mate and they, too, will show you who you are and look at your children, as they too will show you who you are. Or at the very least the people within your life will show you who you were. Now, with that being said, if you are going to do different things within your life then that requires you to widen your circle. You will have to begin incorporating different types of people, places, and things that reflect your new set of ideals. On the path to true success, everybody can't and don't want to come with you. You can't just say you are about that life you have to be about it, regardless of who else is or is not.

If you see yourself as a lawyer and you are currently a

mother/father, a janitor, a high school/college student, or simply someone who is changing careers then you have to set yourself up on the path to law school. You won't be able to practice law just because you have the desire. You have to drop the magazines and/or comics for law journals. You don't have to go cold turkey but you do have to make space to incorporate these other things in your life that will put and keep you on your path. So, instead of dropping the video game, time with friends or other activities just spend less time on them. Use the freed-up time to read up on your new sought-out profession. Go to some public court cases and talk with some lawyers, so you can get at inside perspective to see if it's really what you want.

The point is that when you do decide on what you really want, you will have to entrench yourself into it and let go of anything and everything that does not complement and/or support it. Too many of us let our dreams fall to the waste side because of others and their limitations. As I said before, most of the people in your life reflect something about you, and if it's the limiting part, then you definitely have to let them go. You also have to figure out why are you really unwilling or having difficulty in letting them go. Every person in your life either will be pushing you to your best self or pulling you away from it.

I have a girlfriend, Nicole, who is more like a sister. We have been best friends for more than 15 years, and on first glance, it may seem that we are exact opposites of each other. By this I mean, you can see from your reading what type of person I am, and what I am into. Well, my BFF is not into this stuff as deeply, she is more like everyone else. By that I mean Nicole wants it, but she is not ready to put the work into having it. As you know, I grew up in what we call the hood aka urban cities within America and Nicole reflects that lifestyle, not as bad as most, but it's still there.

Now, with that being said, Nicole has all the ability that I do, and is a natural-born leader as well. However, she is not consistently and relentlessly tapping into that part of herself. We joke that we are each other's alter egos. We also look alike, so everybody always ask us if we are sisters and at this point we just say yes. I love this woman so much. Nicole has always felt like one of my real blood sisters, and my family accepts her as such. Our birthdays are two days apart and at any given moment, we know what each other are thinking. We finish each other's sentences and we can go into the same place at different times, and be attracted or notice the same exact thing. We will call each other up to share it; just to realize that the other one came across it, too and all types of other cool stuff.

We have a very serious bond; it's almost like we are married to each other, but it's nothing at all romantic; purely spiritual. As I write this, I am now very clear on why our bond exists and what it means. For one, she is one of my many soul mates. Throughout the years, it always seemed like I have been teaching her but Nicole has been teaching me just as equally. By this, I mean the aggression that my friend holds and the rough edges that she has are the same exact ones that I have acknowledged within myself. It has only been through our relationship, that I was able to recognize these things within myself. Which allowed me to decipher between whether I approved or disapproved them, and ultimately gained the power to change them. My sister girlfriend unbeknownst to me or her at the time has always has been a mirror for me.

Nicole reflected who I was under the makeup, the titles and the quest for greatness. Through her and only her, I was able to accept and change the parts of me that I wanted to get rid of. Although throughout our friendship, I always felt like it was one-sided that I was constantly giving, and Nicole was constantly receiving. Most times that was true, but I understood that my friend was an only child at least in her mother's house, so she had a selfish bone. Nicole never had to worry about others unlike me with the mommy bone, because that's all I ever did was worry about others.

So my friend always would promise to do better, be more supportive of me, as well as step her game up in her own life. I would accept that, and be understanding of it, as I knew who we both were. Although every now and again, we would get into those deep arguments, and Nicole would say, "well, if I am so bad, why are you my friend?" I would always with tears in my eyes mirroring the ones in hers, say, "because you are I and I need you in my life." Which was the truth, but when I would try to really break it down, I couldn't find any other words outside of those. I now know that what I was really trying to say is that "I am just as dependent on you as you are on me." See, my friend is the only person who really knows the whole me, Nicole knows me just as well as I know myself, and she was the only person who truly accepted me, regardless.

I have always been my absolute whole self with her. I am a very sexy, crazy, and cool person but most only know me from a one-dimensional perspective. Nicole knows all of my dirty secrets, all my hang-ups, heartbreaks, and my dreams. Nicole never forces me into any one aspect of who I am. Basically what I am saying is outside of revealing some of my truth in this book. Nicole is the only person in my life who I have ever truly trusted with the full depth of my mind. Nicole is my safe place in my life; she has never betrayed my trust and I love her so much for that. When I think about the significance of such, it truly knocks everything else out of the window. It reveals her extreme importance in my life because to have a relationship such as that with anyone is a true blessing. That's another reason why she is more than a friend; she is my sister.

Now as my life began to transform in the same ways as yours is about to, I knew that, as my best friend, Nicole, was not coming with me. I had to let her go as the more I held onto her in that capacity, the more I pushed the friendship that I really needed away. By this, I mean we are definitely sisters, for life, but as best friends, Nicole was not meeting the requirements of the job. While I continued to try to Play-Doh her and be frustrated with the results, I was blocking out any potential friendships with other women who could have been the one or the ones, I so desperately needed. You must understand that two exact forces cannot occupy the same space at the same time. So, I was never going to obtain the friendship I was looking for by constantly trying to fix the one I was currently in.

It's the same thing when it comes to romantic love; you are not going to be with the one who you really want to be with by simply getting up every day and being with the one who wants to be with you. At some point, you have to choose, as it's truly unfair to everyone. I couldn't keep hurting and settling for less, because I didn't have the support I needed. I couldn't keep forcing those requirements on my sister girlfriend as I knew at that time she was incapable of giving me those elements. Nicole, would hurt, feel guilt, be ashamed, and would feel not good enough because she wanted to but she didn't have what I needed for herself; let alone for me. I also couldn't keep pushing the other women away in my potential friendships, as they never were really given the opportunity to flourish, because I was so busy caught up in her that I was constantly rejecting them. Understand that leaving things behind or rearranging them is sometimes all the growth you ever need.

What impact does my removing these things have on others?

There is nothing in your life that you do or don't do that won't affect others. Some will be open to your changes, and some will not be, but at the end of the day, you can't worry about that, as it's not going to get you where you are trying to go. Therefore, there will be those in your life who will benefit greatly from your newfound way of living. If you have any children or are interacting with any, they will finally get to meet the better version of you, and they will learn from what they see you doing. As the old saying goes, children do not really listen to what you say as much as they pay attention to what you do. That's where they really learn how to react, how to be, and how to live.

So when you are detoxifying your life of people, places, and things that don't serve you well in the direction that you currently are going, you are also for better or worse teaching others around you how to do it as well. For instance, by me accepting Nicole completely for who she was and being honest that I need more. As well as, releasing her from the bondage of my ideal friendship. I was able to clearly see who she really was to me and why I loved her so much, which allowed me to appreciate her more greatly for that.

For Nicole, the benefits are the release of pressure and guilt, knowing that she doesn't have to be that person I needed her to be or do those things. As I love her unconditionally just as she had always loved me. We are lifetime partners, and I am no longer there in her life being a blessing blocker. Which will ensure that she is guided in her life by God's voice and not mine. Also now my other girlfriends finally have my attention, and I am receiving friendships that are mutually beneficial in my life. So, yes, the entire experience has been hard but at the end of the day, we are in a better place because of it.

What you are about to go through is an amazing journey of self-discovery. It is going to feel like you are in a movie. One of those movies like "The Pursuit of Happyness," "Into the Wild," "Rocky IV," "Seven Pounds, "A Beautiful Mind," "Eat Love Pray," and "The Secret Life of Walter Mitty." If you never have seen any of these movies, then you should definitely pull up your Netflix. Better yet, you need to purchase original copies of these, as they will be worth watching and watching again. If you have or have not seen these movies, and are wondering what this journey looks and feels like, then these movies are your absolute best visual depiction of what you will go through and how you will come out.

You will find yourself just like each of the main characters, watching this riveting, head-turning, scene-by-scene drama known to you as your life that you are the writer, director, producer, and star within. They will not leave you the same after you experience them. This will truly be a surreal experience, as your journey will reflect your evolution in motion. Who needs Darwin, when you have you a true-life story?

I don't know everything, nor do I desire to, but I do know what I know. As I write this book, I too am going through the process. The writing of this book in it-self is a part of my journey. As I write, I am crying, I am thinking, I am challenging, I am detoxing, and I am gain-ing greater understanding about myself. This process is providing me with actualizing astronomical amounts, of encouraging momentum to keep pushing beyond my own fears. The challenges will be many, both large and small, as each day you will have to push yourself beyond your normal. Even in this very moment as I type these thoughts, I am being challenged. It's 1:30 a.m., I am sick and my whole body aches.

I have tissue sticking out of both nostrils, Vicks on my chest, I have chills throughout my whole body, my throat is sore, my head feels like a huge bowling ball, and I had an argument with my husband earlier this evening. I could have abandoned my daily writing goal, or I could have just as I did pushed forward. When I set a goal, my intent is to accomplish it, and to overcome any challenge put in my way to do so. Most likely, I probably still will be sick in the morning, and I have to face this very same challenge again, but I will also feel proud and accomplished, because I continued on and that's how you obtain real esteem.

Things like that tell you who you really are, without the accolades; it's just you vs. you! However, through-out my personal journey, there are some days when I am not so strong. I just stay in bed all day; silently cry to myself, secretly screaming and sobbing like a moth-erless child, because I want it all so bad right now. So much so that sometimes it even physically hurts! You too will probably have days like that, as well, but you must know it's ok, and a part of the journey. You just can't get stuck in there! Now, when God gives me the next day after the hard day, as He will give to you I, just like you, will be back up and on it. Even your pain has great purpose, and it will give you strength to carry on. So let pains processes unfold, but understand the key is that you can never stay wallowing within it.

For me personally, I want to be the best me I could possibly be which is the very me that God intended. I also want to be loved, understood, supported, and respected for it. I to want to unapologetically come into unison with my complete self. I want to explore, challenge, evolve and be a part of the goodness of the world. I want to forever live my best life. It took me 33 years to get where I am, and I am sure it won't take that long to get where I am going. However, it will take time and I am ready to spend my life investing that time. Are you, willing to do that? What is it that you want?

Understand that you are not alone as we are in this thing we call life together. Most of us are experiencing the same things in one form or another. I know these things because I too am going through them. I see the great difference that they are making in my own life. My life in every aspect is opening up more and more in the ways that I desire most and yours can too, but you must be willing to do the work. If you are still a little confused about how your changes as an individual will impact others than just think about how my changes as an individual are impacting you right now in this moment. Give back to the world by giving back to yourself. One person does make all the difference.

CHAPTER FOUR

DEVELOP YOUR REALITY FROM WITHIN

"Build a big enough buzz, so that it comes to you! You can't always chase it down, but you have to do the work, as it doesn't just happen."

Russell Simmons, Business Magnate

Remember in chapter two when I said I wanted peace in my life? Overall, I am a very peaceful person to the point that most people who know me best or know of me would probably say; "she is really great," "very positive – the peacemaker." However, they also would say, "but you don't want to get on her bad side, as her wrath is just as strong." All true, but I was living and grew up in an area that was anything but peaceful. Every night, I would fall asleep to the sounds of sirens and people I knew, or that were two degrees of separation from me were dying daily. Then on top of all of that, I was an activist, an entrepreneur, a photographer, a community leader, and a motivational speaker. So, I constantly would be placing myself in hostile environments trying my best to uplift folks. I got up daily with the goal of being a light in a sea of darkness.

I know that I reached plenty of folks, but the job was never easy, and at the end of it all, the psychological effects started to take a toll on me. It was very clear that the desire for peace was never going to be obtained for me in Newark, New Jersey. No matter how many red carpets, political functions, celebrity encounters, networking events, upscale lounges, beautiful art galleries, nonprofits, community events, and all that any big metropolis city had to offer, the peace I needed just wasn't on the menu. So, I could have given up on my ideal life right then and there, because everybody knew how much Realism Hargrave loved Newark; however I didn't give it up. I gave Newark up because I loved me more. Sometimes letting go is not only your last option, it's your absolute best option.

After radically detoxifying my life, which included relocating from New Jersey to the greater Atlanta area; ending relationships; leaving money, recognition, my company, Newark Press and Co., access, and prominent projects on the table as well as a mentality that was no longer serving my best interest. I found myself to really be alone. I felt alone in the past, but this was a different type of alone; this was isolation. Outside of my husband and my children, as well as my immediate family back home, I pretty much isolated myself from everyone for a few months.

As you will come to find out, when you are on a path to greatness, you have no time for goodness or anything below it. You don't want to hear about the old stuff you used to hear about. You don't want to talk about the old stuff you used to talk about. You don't want to see the people you used to see, and you don't want to go to the places you used to go. This is because you have to set yourself a part from all the things that used to be for all the things that will be. See, the people, places, and things in our lives reflect us, so if you want something different, most likely you will not obtain it with them because they are okay where they are.

They won't be interested in what you are talking about. They won't participate in what you want to participate in because it's not for them at that time. You will find yourself feeling frustrated and rejected. They will say things to you like; "you changed, you think you are better than, and a whole bunch of other nonsense." It will hurt, but the truth is you did change you are better than you were before and they can see and feel it. So some will be angry, but so what! They won't call and they won't support because they will feel left behind.

This does not mean you have to leave where you are, but for me I had to, as I mentally could not take it. God told me to leave, so I did. Now without all the fuzz in the air surrounding or rather suffocating you; you then will have an opportunity to really breathe. An opportunity to go even deeper, and ask yourself these questions; what do I really want in my life, who am I, am I capable of welcoming change, and how bad do I want it? Trust me by the time you get to this point, you will have the answers as you already will have accomplished so much that your answers will start to just drop in your head like clues.

Each clue will lead you to the next and then to another. Things will begin to make sense to you about your life, and how it has developed thus far. You will see that nothing just happened to you and it all had purpose. For me, I knew who I was, I knew what I wanted, and I knew that I wasn't going to get it there. Professionally, my job was about telling and advocating other people's stories via photography, interviews, social media, public relations, activism, and more. On a small scale, I was very much like Central Newark's very own Oprah Winfrey, without the money, of course, which essentially was my dream.

Oprah Winfrey had been my longtime idol. It was the vision of her that birthed my dream. As a little girl when I saw her on TV changing people's lives and encouraging them, I knew that's exactly what I wanted to do with my life. I wanted to be just like her, and to do exactly what she did. I even felt I had an edge on her, because her life pretty much unfolded to be what it is, whereas for me she was my template. So I knew exactly what path I would take to get there, but my blessing and curse were that I believed in lifting others as I climbed.

I was always giving people an opportunity to be who they wanted to be. Shining a light on them and the problem with that was that the more I moved forward, the more I would look backward. Therefore, I wasn't getting where I really wanted to be, because I was spending so much time worrying about others getting there, too. I knew that my next step was to stop telling other people's stories and to start telling my own.

I never was going to be seen for what my real value was because I was too busy showcasing the value of others. People would become attracted to me through the media piece of my business; the DSLRs, the microphones, the press passes, the hosting, the websites, the videos, the magazines, the other freelance photography and social media, but they would stay with me because of the empowerment, the love, and my exhilarating energy. I did so many things, all community- and communications-based, that people knew me for a lot of things and yes, that was cool, but it had a downside. The downside was that the one thing that I really wanted to be was the last thing I was being recognized for.

I am an Indigo Child, or what some call a light worker,

and as such, I am a gifted messenger put on earth to restore souls. God has given me the gifts of vast insight, compassion, prophecy, empathy, awareness, and the ability to assist in the evolving and healing of the world by helping others become whole through my insightful and passionate messages and leadership. Ok, don't freak out like; did she just say that? Yes, I did, as it's my whole truth. I know exactly who I am, and this entire process will help you to find out exactly who you are, if you don't already know, and it will allow you to accelerate your path into being it.

I used the media to empower people by providing a necessary resource within my community in hopes that others would see the great people around them and become inspired by the possibilities within their own lives. Everything I did was on a positive note, so while the body counts kept rising, I kept providing an alternative view of the people, places, and things within Newark, NJ. People loved me for it, and always wanted me to be everywhere. I never paid for things, and I received more invites than I could ever possibly attend and everybody wanted to be on my radar whether they secretly hated me or not.

I had the ear of the people, and if anybody was doing anything, they wanted me there on the scene at the scene when the scene was being seen. Some of you may be thinking, "well, you were the media and who doesn't want the media to be there, highlighting their accomplishments?" However, it was more than that as I always had interns, volunteers, freelancers, etc. but they wanted me specifically because my energy would become the cherry on top.

If I was there, then the people who weren't would know all about it, and the people who were there would feel important, like celebrities themselves. People always would talk about me to the organizers as one of the factors that increased how great of a time they had. The reason for this, and I am not bragging, was because that was my intention. I wanted people to feel good. I wanted people to see their neighbors living and enjoying life. I never reported on the negative, although I would personally rally, protest, and advocate against it, while partnering with many nonprofits and do-gooders, on plenty of diverse solution-based projects and initiatives.

In addition to all that, because I was a community person, my entire brand was built on truth and integrity. If I said something about you or was with you, it was an endorsement. The people who were in my audience trusted me as the source, so they in turn trusted you as the subject. That's why I was selective, because I didn't do anything with anyone or for anyone that I didn't believe in, and I wasn't one of those chasers. I knew my worth, so I was not trying to be anywhere and everywhere some big name was.

As the city and world grew crazier and crazier by the minute, I had another decision to make, which was whether I was going to get sucked up into it or was I going to cut through the BS and get folks back on track. I knew that the time had come that I had to come from behind the camera, behind the microphone, and start really giving it to the people directly from within me. That's when I decided to write this book, and rebrand my business "Newark Press" from a media, communications, and marketing company to "Realism Hargrave Communications" a life empowerment agency. I decided that the next half of my life had to begin right now. That I had to do exactly what I was created to do. No more coming in from the back door.

This is a choice that you too will have to make at some point, whose side are you on? Will you contribute to peace and prosperity on earth, or will you succumb to the negativity and perpetuate it? Again, you don't have to become the next MLK, you just got to become the first you as that's really enough right there. The more you that you become, the more you will be lead with ease to the next steps of your life. Becoming you will not simply happen by reading this book. You have to live out this book! You have to actually do the work on you, and then do it again and again, until you are actually become it.

Starting to Live Your Best Life Now will be a daily decision that you will have to make until it becomes as normal as putting on your socks or stockings in the morning. At that time, it will no longer be a decision or a challenge, as it will simply become your way of life. Some changes will be able to be implemented immediately, and others will take more time. However, as long as you are working on it, then they too will come to pass. No delays, take action today, even in the smallest way possible.

What do I need to do to really begin living my new reality?

Stop for a minute and think about the world outside of you; think about the people you come across; think about the TV shows, the music, and the news; more importantly, think about the children. I'm sure your head is shaking up and down, as many of us are in a very bad state, and think about how many pleasant people you come across in relation to how many unpleasant people you come across. Or maybe they are not unpleasant at all, but they are clearly unhappy, whether it is because of their job, their career, their marriage, their relationships, and/or just themselves. I always knew that the world's most serious problem is the fact that people are not being who they were designed to be.

Everything is out of whack it's like using a hammer to unscrew something or trying to put a square peg into a circle hole. Those are all very defeating. Think about what you yourself are attracted to. What gets your attention, what are your social media posts about, what's in your iPod, what gets a rise out of you, and what are you focusing your attention on? Most of us are not happy, as we have been taught to pretend to be because happiness means and looks the same thing for all of us! That is the stupidest thing I have ever heard. Happiness is just like life; it's not a one-size-fits-all deal. So why are you perpetuating this belief? We believe that the world, and everything else in it, is complete. We believe that we are just fighting amongst each other to get a piece of it. That's all wrong, as we are the piece that the world needs!

Life is constantly evolving, and that's why each generation is always better than the last, as they too have a job to do. Children are not just burdens or responsibilities, they also have come to teach, learn, and contribute. Everything we do and don't do, down to the smallest part, matters. The point that I am making is that we all have a role to play, and most of us are not doing our part. We have all been lied to, as it is not the institution that is great; it is the people whom make up the institution whom are great. Imagine a life where you felt important and accounted for? Where you knew that the work you were doing had meaning greater than just someone else getting rich. For the sake of the survival of humanity; life is not simply about surviving it is about living!

Great living requires you to take chances, face obstacles, seize opportunities, and not let your ego, hate, and/or fear limit the possibilities of your life. You must recognize that you are a spiritual being having a human experience. Your feelings act as a guide from your spiritual self, instructing you on which way to go and who to go with. Revealing visions to you known as dreams that expose the possibilities of your life. If you follow the path that your intuition is eagerly instructing you to take, you will always be in a state of becoming. You will understand that everything that happens to you is necessary to get you to whom God has selected you to be. To a place where you are excitedly playing your role and making a contribution to the world's becoming, as it too is not complete.

Remember the person I mentioned earlier who I fell in love with? My meeting MT had a dramatic affect on me and my relationship with him has been significantly trying. He changed my life upon our meeting and his presence in my life literally woke me up by closing the gap between my soul and myself. This unanticipated meeting ended the saga of my double life. My double-life syndrome was based off of the two separate realities that I was living. The two realities reflected one on the outside who was living the so-called dream and the one on the inside who was still dreaming. In my best interest MT has made some personal sacrifices for me; revealing a certain type of love that I had not experienced before.

I never felt more protected or loved by a man. No one ever stuck their own neck out for me, by considering what was in my best interest over their very own. The level of strength displayed by MT astounded me, as this is the role I normally play in my relationships. It really felt amazing although painful at times, to have someone do these things for me. He willingly had given up some level of his own personal happiness for my ultimate wellbeing, which is very similar to what I have been doing my whole life for others. However, it would be very superficial of me to believe all that was just done for me. MT has a great sense of awareness and respect for himself and although he is very strong; in my eyes, like most I believe him to be very fearful as well.

Therefore, it would be naive of me to believe that his decisions were made solely for my wellbeing and not at all for his self-preservation. Yes, it does sound both upstanding and crazy. The full understanding of this circumstance is complex and was greater than my mind would allow. As only after years into it am I, finally gaining some level of understanding about it.

Now I appreciate all that, because obviously when I first met him in 2009, I needed it. However, as time went on, it became painfully clear to me that I needed MT to be more active in my life. As his presence on any level makes me better. There is just something about him that illuminates me. Understand that everything is not of a romantic nature, and when God brings people together so significantly, it is a sin not to acknowledge or respect it. It's like having someone to help you create, and although you can create on your own, this person's assistance makes your creations much more profound. Their participation within your creation is the clear difference between being good and being great. In my eyes, I wonder why people settle for good, when great is a viable option?

Life is about constant elevation; you don't walk up a few stairs and just stay there, you keep going until you get to the floor you were looking for. At this point in my eyes the perpetuation of such illusive decisions by him seem to be nothing more than cowardly. They are clearly not based off of love they are based off of extreme fear. Or to be fare, since I do not truthfully know maybe they are genius based off a higher level of understanding of some kind that is unbeknownst to me. However, I do know that God does not give you the ability to impact people, so that you don't impact them. He gives you that power so that you can. If you don't use the power, talent, gift that God has given you, then you are ultimately contributing to the imbalance of the world.

The point is that most of you are like MT. You sit on your very own gifts, while searching for your purpose; which is right there staring you in the face. You say you are a person of faith, but you do not act upon your faith. You foolishly deny the people, places, and things that God sends to you because you are too afraid to think, to receive, and to love on your own. Your ideals are limited to what the outside world has taught you about what can and cannot be. You have to stop listening to that crap and start following your gut, you have to listen to God's word, you have to recognize your intuition, you have to pursue your art, and you have to love the people that you feel the love for.

Be optimistic and let life guide you rather than you guiding life. Let go of the false sense of control. It does not matter where you currently are in life, those deep-down impressions are telling you where you have to go. If you do not fulfill our own personal missions, you will never feel the completeness or happiness that your hearts desire. Abundance, exhilaration, excitement, and happiness are awaiting you on the other side of your programming. Pain should not be the only emotion that we welcome, allow, respond to, and wallow in. God wants us to be happy, and we can and we will be, but we have to stop the mask wearing in the areas of our lives that forecast who we really are. Faith is an action word, and you have to most times abandon what you know for what you don't to truly express it.

Your life is too important to be living a lie or living in the shadows of your fear, potential, and possibility. If your, mere presence or interaction with someone can help them to be their greatest self, then who are you to reject such influence? If your, song can change the hearts of anyone who heard it, then who are you not to write it? If your, love could help someone build or change a nation, then who are you to withhold it? If your smile can dry up a rainy day, then who are you not to show it? If your, insight has the ability to restore souls for the betterment of mankind, then who are you not to give it? What does your life matter without doing so anyway?

This is where your happiness lies, inside of those deep-down feelings inside. Imprisoned behind the superficial elements of your everyday life. You have to believe that your life means more than wanting, desiring, and trying to figure it out. You already really know what your purpose is. Just take a deeper look as it has always been with you, struggling to make an appearance. Trapped underneath the junk, behind the false ideals of what life is supposed to be, behind what making it looks like, behind what success is, and behind the fear. So many of us are out there getting up every day and making moves based on what they are going to say, what they are going to do, and what they are thinking!

Shut the noise out, and live your life, follow your heart, let your intuition, which is your direct connect to your higher self and God guide you for the rest of your days. The happiness you seek is within your reluctance to play your position just as the displacement you have been feeling is within your willingness to spend your life trying to find the answers that are already within.

These answers are lying dormant inside of you because you like most lack the courage to act upon them.

Will implementing these changes be easy or trying at times?

Nothing worth having comes easy, especially when you are deprogramming and reprogramming throughout the process. It's the actual undoing that is the hardest part. It's basically like teaching an old dog new tricks; your body, your mind, and everything else around you has been programmed in a certain way, and now you have to deprogram it. This means that you are going to be challenging yourself constantly to do and be different. These challenges may be as simple as taking more baths and fewer showers to obtain more personal time to think; or they will be medium, such as incorporating more exercise in your life; or they may be large, like quitting your job; or huge ones, like getting a divorce. No matter how big or small they will all take time to incorporate and some will take more time than others, and you have to be patient about these things.

Respect the process and remember the decision to do it in itself is hard enough. So you can't be in haste, as some things will take a bit more planning than others. You have to set reasonable goals for yourself, and you have to let go of expectation. I spoke about this early on when I discussed the need to control things. Don't try to control the outcome or the process. Just control the commitment to it, because honestly, that's all you can control. Make the choice and the commitment to do this or that. Keep the commitment to stay diligently on your path. Control the commitment to stay focused and to stay strong. Then just continue with the commitment, regardless of the cost. It will be painful at times, as difficult decisions will have to be made, and it will be challenging, because it's unlike anything you have ever done before. Understand you are transforming yourself and your life from the inside out.

Those transformations one after another will lead you to the next, and they will make it clear to you when the time is now for the next one to unfold. The more transformed that you find yourself to be the more you will see your life unfolding in the manner that you desire. When I began to transform my life, I noticed that my tolerance level for things was adjusting between two extremes. I was becoming more patient and more accepting of some things, and then, on the other end, I was becoming less and less tolerant of others.

The intolerance was for simple things, such as certain conversations, things on TV, particular attitudes and mindsets or simply people's behaviors. It was either things that may have bothered me before did not anymore, or some things that did bothered me before, bothered me even greater now. I refused to put myself in situations that didn't make me feel good. So if talking to you at that particular time was going to put me in a negative disposition; creating worry or frustration, then I wasn't going to talk to you.

It did not matter how many times you called, emailed, or text, I was no longer willing to put out fires at my own expense. By this I mean, I was no longer willing to sacrifice my very own emotional wellbeing for someone else. I have always been putting the needs of others before my own and part of my work in starting to live my best life now is to learn how to choose me and put me first. This ensures my health and my ability to truly assist others. You must be conscious about the energy that you are giving to things. We are not God & we are not an overflowing and everlasting source of energy. Therefore ours can actually drain out, so you must be selective in who and what you choose to give it to.

My motto now regarding this is to simply do what you can, when you can, where you can. So, I would unapologetically give you a call if and when I was ready or not at all. I was no longer willing to allow others to capitalize off of my time, no longer willing to negotiate my fees for my work for lesser value than they were worth, and I was no longer willing to offer more than I could at the time. If I needed time alone or off I was taking it, and whatever the consequences were of that, then I would accept them. Don't waste your time on idle minds and things. If it's not feeding you in some way, then you shouldn't constantly be feeding it!

Starting to live your best life now is simply about doing the things that give you the greatest amounts of satisfaction in the present moment. It's about making everyday decisions that feel good, bring joy, excitement and enrichment into your life. It's about spending time with friends you enjoy; who actually contribute to your life. These are not the friends that you have to babysit their behavior or are always the Debbie or Don Downer in the room. You can't really enjoy yourself with these types of people! As most likely you are spending your time constantly asking them if they are alright or you are cringing every time the life of the party gets up, because you are afraid of what they are going to say or do next.

It is not about arguing with someone every day; trying to transform them into the person you want them to be in your life. It's not about doing things day after day and year after year that you absolutely hate. It's not about accepting any less than what you are worth! It's about each day making conscious decisions based upon the joy or pleasure that you seek. It's about spending your time with people who increase your being. It's like making an investment, which provides you with a return of another great day. There is no worrying about yesterday, the rest of today, or tomorrow; it's about experiencing "now" from moment to moment and having the faith to know that God is guiding you step by step.

So live! Stop wasting the moments within your life and begin to embrace, appreciate and curate them. If you are going to be more happy dropping those 20 pounds, then you better get your butt in the gym, and you better become more conscious about what you are putting into your mouth. You will need support to keep momentum, so whether that is developing a friendship with someone who is into fitness and health or going to social media for inspiration. You have to make the commitment to do something. You must surround yourself with people, places, and things that make it easy to stay on track.

If those around you don't share your mindset than your work is to attract those into your life who do. This attracting is not achieved by simply wishing; it is only achieved by vigorously doing. Filling yourself up with the necessary elements to be and to obtain what you want will be the defining factors of whether or not you receive them into your life. What you actualize into your life reflects who and where you are within your life. So if you are obtaining the very things you don't want than this is because you are attracting them. Always remember that these things and the experiences you are having are mirroring where you currently are.

Maintain balance in your life in everything you do. So maybe eat right five days out of the week, and live a little for the other two or whatever works for you. This way, you reward yourself, instead of setting yourself up for

failure by being extreme. Remember, you are not looking for a quick diet; these are long-term lifestyle changes.
Your start living your best life now success depends on
you being specific and strategic in your life. Figure out
exactly what you want, develop strategies on how to obtain it and do the necessary work.

Keep in mind that the above formula is the blueprint
for all of the areas in your life, and not just one. That, too,
is where the difficulty comes into play, because you are
implementing these methods in several areas of your life
simultaneously. No one area in your life is so great that
it will compensate for all the other areas. Starting to live
your best life now is about increasing the quality of your
life and being great in a holistic and cohesive manner.

How will these changes impact others around me?

When you desire something or someone to be a certain way, then most of us try to Play-Doh the situation
or the person. Basically we hopefully mold it or them
into what we want, and most times it never happens; or
it's a temporary fix. The reason being is that we barely
can control ourselves, let alone others. When we try, this
is where the major problems unfold, because people are
people, and for better or worse, they are going to do what
they want to do. They just like you cannot escape from
being whom and what they are and there is nothing that
anyone outside of them can do about it. Throughout my
years of being a community servant as well as via my
marriage, I have learned this the hard way, and even today I still struggle with it.

The people that I love the most I can't just throw them
away, so I always try to religiously work on the issues.
Hoping that we would come to some sort of middle
ground. It never worked, because people are so ego-

focused on being right and they are fearful of being attached to anything that they feel has a negative connotation. The reality, even more so than the above is that; if it's not who they are then it's just not. You have to accept that reality and seek out those in your life who are what you desire. So for me personally I am currently done with that strategy; it's in full retirement.

I realized if you want someone to change or someone wants you to change then that's your key that you are dealing with the wrong person for that position. The person you truly want, won't need to change as they simply just are what you where looking for and vice versa. Now mind you sometimes they were or you were but if it is no longer than that in itself is another key that is time to move on from that relationship. This little nugget goes for all areas of our relationships regardless if they are platonic, romantic or professional. In the past I always tried to do it anyway which taught me what I know now. Once I would have finally exhausted myself from trying to mold someone or a relationship, I would then unapologetically be done and there was no returning. Although, I am a work horse so this level of exhaustion did not come easy as I would toil for years with the people I love, believe in or just wanted in my life for some reason.

As I write this, I have just realized that I really used to do this for me and not for them or us, as I once believed. By this I mean I wanted to ensure for my own conscious and servitude that I tried my absolute best to make it work. What I have learned is that like it or not, you have to lovingly let this people be; stop wasting both of your time. That does in some cases and does not in others mean they are no longer in your life. At the very least you may have to put them in a less important or more appropriate role. That way you both don't have the same unwanted affect on each other as you use to. People are not bad, it's just that everything is not compatible with everything and sometimes the compatibility that use to be there, no longer exist.

So you find yourselves at war with people about the essence of them. Meaning the differences of ideas, values, ways etc, when in actuality your relationships should for the most part be one of ease and not disease. Therefore, just as all of your other changes you make, for some they will be impacted greatly as you are bringing a new level of enlightenment into their lives. For others they will do their damnedest to stop your progress, as they don't want you to grow and leave them behind. Although, you will have to do what you have to do for them and yourselves. Someone has to be the courageous one, as the last thing you need is deadweight, and the last thing any person needs is to feel less than.

When it comes to others in your life, your signal of knowing when something is good is; if it is easy, then it is right, and if it is not easy, then it is wrong. If it started easy, then it was right at that time and if it is no longer easy, it is because it is no longer right at this time. You will have to release those who stand in the way of your true happiness. It does not mean you hate them or they are no good, it just means that their part in your story has come to an end. This is the troublesome part because it is much easier to say let them go, than it is to actually do it. However, you have to decide who is more important them or you?

The good news is that it will free you up to attract via your energy those who will complement you and those who can appreciate and respect you for where you are now. Your most important two relationships are the one with God and the one with yourself, and all others are irrelevant when it comes to the two; even your marriage and your children. By this I mean, if you are not healthy in those departments, then you are seriously malnourished in the others. Therefore, you are not bringing anything to the table that is really worth having.

Without developing those two relationships you are falling extremely short of what you could be contributing to anyone. With constant development of those two relationships, you will give greatly, you will live richly and you will inspire. More importantly, when you are in a healthy and happy state, your vibration goes out and unto the earth. You will fill in more of that white, which is interpreted as peace in the yin-yang symbol. Your personal happiness actually helps harmonize and balance the universe's overall life force.

This is the-higher-self stuff that matters much more than the-lower-self things that we just spoke about. Your vibrations through your energy levels, for better or worse, have an affect on the entire world! Remember when we spoke earlier about looking at the world around us, the TV, the music etc? I think we both agreed that things are out of whack, but this vibration we are speaking about helps things on a universal level get back on track. The more of us who are actually living our best lives now through God, then the more momentum the world will have to whip itself back into shape.

I know for some of you, you may be like; "hey, she is losing me here with this worldly talk," but this is the very foundation of start living your best life now. It's simply about you being your best and leading the highest quality of life possible for yourself. By following your gut, which is your direct connect to God. These actions by you will directly assist the world into developing at its optimum prime. Think of it in this way; the body gets bruised and because it is full of nutrition and all the parts of it are working, as it should, the body then rapidly heals itself with no need for a doctor or any foreign substances. Now imagine the world as the actual body itself, you as one of the working parts, and your happiness and its energy that it vibrates as the nutrition.

Now hold that thought and imagine the scenario being the complete opposite, which clearly represents the world's current condition now. The body is bruised, the parts are not working as they should, and therefore they lack the nutrition needed to heal itself. So instead of the body rapidly healing; it is slowly but surely deteriorating due to an otherwise normally mild infection. An infection that is spreading throughout the rest of the body and the body will not survive without some immediate surgery. The point is you greatly matter and your life is bigger than just you! For better or worse, you at your most healthiest and best self are greatly needed within the world.

CHAPTER FIVE

Allow Your New Reality to Unfold

"Always do your best, and that's how you became a master at your craft! No matter what the situation, never make excuses, simply create the circumstances that you want to be."

Doug E. Fresh, Beatboxer, Rapper & Record Producer

After I did all of the emotional and mental work that was needed to desire, define, detox, and develop what it was that I truly wanted and did not want in my life. It was time to begin making the ideals in my ideal life tangible realities. I discovered exactly what I wanted, why I wanted it, who I wanted, who I didn't want, what I didn't want, why I didn't want it, what was blocking me from it, and how to unblock it. To make it even simpler, I knew where I stood and how I got there and what was needed to get me to the next place. Each part of my journey, as each part of yours, will lead you to a greater understanding of yourself, but you can't shortcut or skip. If you do, you will miss something that you will have to confront at some point or another.

So if you are going to transform your life, then you really need to give it your all or just stop here because anything less is a repeat of your current circumstance.

I am sure at this point that you notice that this book is not like any other self-help guide that you have read before, if you have ever read any. This book is a behind the scenes, backstage pass to who you have to be and what you have to go through to really obtain your dreams. It deals with the psychological, spiritual, and emotional perspectives that you have to have not only to accomplish your dreams, but also to live a better quality of life. This newer version of your life will absolutely enhance your overall life experience as well as the world around you.

The Start Living Your Best Life Now ideal is not for the faint at heart and it's not for the guy or gal who wants superiority in one area of their life. This is a holistic method for those who really want to have it all together in every area of their life based upon their own desire and God's will. Those who want it all in the sense of great careers, marriages, relationships, parenting abilities, lifestyle, wealth, spirituality, health, adventure, and whatever else one's heart can fathom.

When I was living my "so-called" dream, that's all I was doing, but I was unsatisfied in many other areas of my life. My actual life was taking a back seat to the demands of the dream. It was as if I signed a contract that said if you want to keep doing this, then you are going to have to give up all of that. All of that included; time for myself, time with my family and friends, time to rediscover and time to pursue my other dreams. More importantly the time to live out my full calling from God.

When I first started building my family, I was fairly young at 21, and rough around the edges. My husband Greg was also but he was 23 and wasn't my husband at the time; we were still boyfriend and girlfriend. I met my husband when I was 13, and he was my first official love, but we just became great friends. I ended up connecting with Lawrence, aka Kaz, at age 15, who was my first real boyfriend and also later became my daughter's father. I finally romantically connected with my husband at the age of 18, shortly after the birth of my daughter, as we were always lovers who were friends since the first day we met. When we got together, everything, of course, was great, but we shared the same group of friends, and were young, so we had our ups and downs, which led to many breakups as well as some heartache.

This time we finally decided to really get it together by removing everybody out of our business, for him to stop running back to his mother's house every time we got into an argument and for us to began planning our lives together. Greg played football all throughout high school, went straight to college, surprisingly dropped out, and began engaging in the street life. However, at this point, he was ready to get his life back on track. I was pretty mature by then when it came to family life, as I had a daughter, was living on my own, working in corporate America, and, of course, my whole life, I was always taking care of others. Although as a young woman I was immature in the sense of being loud, naive and obnoxious at times.

We decided to consummate our commitment to each other and truly make our family complete by having a son. My husband loved my daughter, Biasia, and treated her as his own. However Biasia, was not our love child; she was the love child of Lawrence and I. So we sat her down, as she was about four or five at the time and asked Biasia, how she felt about it. Now I know some of you are like; "what, you asked a 4- or 5-year-old about something like that?" Well, the answer is yes, we did because as I said I was mature in those areas. I didn't want to bring a child into the world that would make the child I currently had feel isolated or that she was not completely a part of the family.

Therefore to me, it was better to consider her feelings and receive her blessing, even though she was so young. The reason being is so that she too felt as though she took part in her brother's creation, which at 16 now, at the time of this writing, and 11 for him, has proved to be true. There was never a moment of jealousy between them, and she takes great pride in Shameek's birth and life. See, those are the things that really matter and prevent family dysfunction, especially when dealing with blended families as we were before the term became popular.

I quit my job, and became a stay-at-home mother and Greg went for some computer technician training. By the time he finished, September 11th happened, which created the Transportation Security Administration, and he ended up getting a position at Newark Airport. The pay was great for a young family of four at that time. I was quite the mother and wife; very active at my Biasia's school, house clean, dinner done, lunches packed, birthday parties, celebrations, get-togethers, and great holidays. Another dream come true, as you have to remember we came from a place where dysfunction was all around, so to be living the way we were together was an accomplishment for us.

Our friends were still out in the streets doing what they knew to do, but we were building and evolving, while inspiring those around us. Everyone we know admires our love and us, because they know the many obstacles we overcame for it. That was all great, but after a few years I begin to get bored, as I wanted more. I begin to feel that my worth was being limited to the house, my husband, and my two children. I always felt that I had great purpose, that I was born to make a difference, and I wanted a great, full life where I could have it all. Unbeknownst to me I wanted to start living my best life now back then.

So, I started getting familiar with the Internet and as I said before, I always was a rebel looking for an alternative way of accomplishing great things or simply living. Every day in between the mundane housework, dropping and picking the kids up, making meals, and planning events, I would be on the computer looking for ways to make money or whatever. Greg also at this time was beginning to fear that his position with the TSA was in jeopardy, because of his past, which ultimately proved right. He also was very stressed between that and his mother taking ill since the birth of our son, as he was dedicated to caring for her. Therefore, he started to play with the idea of going back to school, not just for him but for me, too.

I was not enthusiastic about the idea, as I knew at that time that school wasn't for me. Although I was not completely clear on what was for me at the time. Greg and I are very different in that way, as he values the traditional mainstream ideals of society. He has every right to do so, because for many it has been the most guaranteed path. However, for me, I don't believe in that stuff; I am a do-it-your-own-way type of gal and a questioner of everything. Therefore, I am constantly questioning everything; "who says this and who says that, why do we have to listen to them, why does our marriage have to be like this, and why can't it be what we choose for it to be?"

To make a long story short, I started performing my poetry and winning awards, which gave me a greater sense of self outside of the family. Then we both ended up going to the local community college. Outside of knowing college was not for me at some point in my adult life; growing up I never thought, college was even a possibility for me. I associated college with money and I didn't have any so I figured I was never going but my big sister Isis made it to college and that changed the thought of that and opened the door for the rest of us.

I learned a lot about myself in college and the way I thought about things. I met some great people who I am still in contact with today and college helped me buff some of my ruff edges. However, I hated it the whole time, as it was not for me. I felt that higher education, as a whole was a breeding ground for traditional thinking. I felt that the world needed changing and college was not about that. To me the collegiate system itself does not create innovators it creates predecessors. Overall, I have nothing against college, as within context it is very useful. I am sending my children to college but I do sadly believe that people mistake college as an identity rather than a tool. I found myself constantly undoing the things in my mind that they were teaching me.

Essentially, I took away about 20% and left the other 80% on the table. The only thing I really liked was the social experience. It was exciting to be able to communicate with people, challenge ideals, take a stand, and converse with people who actually wanted something out of their lives. Greg, on the other hand seemed to love it; he was very dedicated. He was juggling school, his job with the TSA as well as being his mother's primary caregiver. I, too, was juggling school, my community initiatives and managing the home. The pressure and the stress of it all began to cause things to become real intense for our relationship. On top of that Greg, soon lost his job as he thought he would do to his past activities.

We came up with a plan to take our savings and to save up every dime of his unemployment outside of the normal monthly household maintenance budget and go into business. We moved from where we were, as we needed more space. His mother ended up moving with us and becoming an investor in the business. So now we were in our mid-twenties, raising our two children, going to school full time, planning to develop a cleaning business, taking care of his mom, and struggling to keep our relationship intact as well as provide food on the table. By the grace of God we did it!

When we were finally ready to fully invest the money, after already registering the cleaning company and purchasing a van for the moving of equipment; I got the idea that we should go left and open up a braiding salon instead. We did just that on my mother's birthday. We were still in school, but we managed to open up a 2,000 square foot, upscale braiding salon with 12 stations. We created partnerships with the African community to obtain braiders, we developed relationships with the Korean community in the area who owned the beauty supply stores, and had them opening up early and providing discounts to service our clients.

S&B Braiding Salon named after our children was pretty productive and profitable. However, I also hated it! We were still in school for one, and to effectively operate the business, one of us had to stop going, which it ended up being me as that was not even an option for Greg. Our relationship at this point was so strained with everything and we weren't even married yet. Yes, I know, what you are thinking. "You guys did all of this and you weren't married yet?" No, we weren't married yet; blame it on growing up hood, as people are together forever before, if they ever get married.

I hated it because first and foremost, braiding is a hustle for the majority of African women who come to the US. It is not something that they actually enjoy greatly it's more like a skill that they have which they use to make a living until something better comes along. On the streets we call that a hustle. I personally didn't feel good about that, as I am very sensitive to people's feelings and emotions and although they never said that to me I could clearly see it for myself. Also I was extremely bored, sitting there watching them braid for hours on end. The customers did not appreciate the level of experience that we were providing based upon the industry's normal standards.

So of course, I wanted out! I didn't care about the money or anything. I was not going to continue experiencing or taking part in all of that. Of course, Greg was pissed and it caused further separation. To make a long story short, we got out of it debt free and had the best teaching experience in business possible. Greg gained employment in the technology field of corporate America based off of his previous training while he finished school. I started being on Youtube, created my next company; We The Peoples Media, then we soon after got married and graduated college.

After graduating, I chose not to continue school, as I knew my husband was going to and the strain of both of us attending school simultaneously was too much. So I began to work in nonprofit, and that's when all hell started breaking loose. Our relationship became worse after the marriage because we no longer had one; school, jobs, kids came first, and by the time all those needs were met, there was no time for anything else. I wanted more out of our lives, and Greg seemed to be content with the way things were. I was making money, but unfulfilled in the position. I became overwhelmed with the issues in my life, within the community at large and then I became sick.

Unbeknownst to me I started to suffer from depression. Once I figured it out, I was determined to beat it. Although, I was feeling abandoned by Greg, who was so focused on everything else, and feeling frustrated with the world in general that I ended up spending almost a year of my life mostly in bed. One day out of the blue, I got a call from Mikki, my old college buddy and she invited me to her sister's launch event. I went just because I really needed to get out and I liked her very much so as well as I had not seen her in a long time. I had so much fun and was completely impressed and inspired by what these young women, Glam and DamitaJo, were doing in the community.

Before that time, outside of myself I never saw a group of young black people taking their lives into their own hands like that. Let alone, young black women in Newark, NJ without sponsorship or any major support. Glam and DamitaJo had developed their very own independently funded entertainment company. I was super impressed and greatly inspired. They had a talent showcase featuring some amazing folks to celebrate the launching of their online radio show Celebrity BLVD. So finally feeling some level of excitement in my life, I ran to Youtube and blew it up. Mind you, up until that point, my Youtube was very focused on the issues within the black community as remember throughout all of this I always was a advocating on behalf of the community. This all lead me to receiving an opportunity with Celebrity BLVD, to do a 10-minute report on the radio in or out of the studio about what was going on in the community.

I was so elated, as I truly needed this opportunity in my life especially at that time. It was always a dream of mine to be on the radio and to ultimately one day have my own nationally syndicated radio show. Therefore I was all for it as this is exactly what I needed desperately. At this point, I am about 28 years old, and I did that report like it was nobody's business. I always had a radio voice, as it's captivating, passionate, and exciting. When I first did it, I just did it over the phone, but, of course, I wanted to be in the studio. So the next time I did it in the studio and I met the owner who fell in love with me and gave me an opportunity right then and there. The opportunity involved me co-hosting a show every Tuesday afternoon alongside DJ, Allen, who enjoyed spinning but didn't like to talk.

So, of course, I took that opportunity and did that show until the DJ moved on. At that time the owner offered me the slot and "Real Talkz" was born. From there, I ended up producing and hosting my own radio show with some great friends Tumba, Saffiyah, Uninvited, and Ky. Soon I was simultaneously producing another show featuring three young male DJs, "The TrackStarz", and after about a year I was kicked off of the air for no apparent reason at all. Then, I just went back to doing what I did best, which was my own thing; started two more companies, the short lived Hargrave, Butler & Wilkerson, a public relations and media production company, then ultimately, Newark Press & Co. a multimedia corporation and the rest from there is history.

How do I easily implement all the new changes in my new life?

If you notice through my story, one thing always lead

me to another; for each triumph it lead me to some adversity, and each adversity lead me to another opportunity for growth. If I chose to ignore the feelings that I was having inside, I would have reacted differently in all of the situations and most likely remained within them. I always have been one who has constantly changed the game for herself. So those who witness it are always impressed, but I know that I am just doing what I am supposed to be doing. However, if I had got caught up in other people's perspectives of me or allowed my ego to lead my life, I never would have been capable of pushing past good for better.

Many of us imprison ourselves in the social statuses of our lives; we are living in the shadows of our reputations, rather than being led and being true to our character. As you allow your life to unfold on your journey to greatness, you will see that the map is and has always been inside of you. Greatness is not a straight path of ease and joy, it is a zigzagging path of constant failure and triumph. Once you get to one level, then there is a great big wall up preventing you to get to the next. You will have to break this wall down, and many times, there will be no blueprints available for you.

So you might have to use your body by crashing up and down it until it starts to break, then you will have to use your hands and feet to punch and kick the rest of it out. You either will break a hole big enough for you to climb through or you will knock it completely down. Therefore when it comes to easily allowing your new reality to unfold you have to constantly deprogram your mind. You have to go right when you would normally go left, you have to rely on your intuition when you normally would rely on your mind, and you have to continue when you normally would quit.

I could have easily buckled on every level of my life, beginning with my childhood circumstances. I could have accepted that I never could be great. I could have adopted the mindset that my life would mean nothing to anyone and took one of the obvious doom-and-gloom routes. However, I refused for that to be my truth and if I didn't, we would not be having this engagement with each other right now. As I too would be one of those people just living in the shadows of my dreams and wishing for better days ahead. Don't ever wait for tomorrow to do what you can do today.

At this point, there is nothing to it, but to do it! Since you have identified the changes that you need to make, now it's the time to make them. Your first tangible steps begin at this point. You have removed the distractions, and now it's only left to you. Whatever your goals are, you have to begin implementing them into your life by taking serious action as soon as possible. If you are delaying them even by a day, then you are proving to yourself that you are not serious. You have to make your next move your best move and the one after that even better. You have to make decisions every moment of every day that coincide with your goals.

You have to surround yourself with positive momentum that encourages you along your journey. You have to see the things around you in a whole new light, constantly deciphering what is good and what is not based upon your feelings about it. You have to challenge your every thought and ask yourself why am I doing this or that? Is this good for my goals and me? If you pick up an apple and something inside of you says go for an orange, then you need to let go of that apple and pick up that orange.

The reason being is that there is something about that

orange that is for you at that very moment. Each time that you follow your gut, you will be more aligned with the proper direction of your life. Obviously you are tired of waiting for something to happen, so you must get up and make something happen. You have to entrench your mind, body, and soul with the things that you want to have and to be. If you are waiting for an opportunity to come to you, then most likely you are still waiting.

You have to challenge yourself to be greater than in every aspect of your life. It will not be easy at times, because depending on your situation, you may have to knock down some walls that you yourself created. You have to be honest with yourself by looking yourself in the mirror and, for better or worse, clearly accept who is staring back at you. You have to find the courage within to apologize to those who you have deeply offended, repair the relationships of those whom you have broken.

If something is bothering or haunting you, then you have to address it, no more running and no more ignoring. You have to forgive yourself for the wrongs that you have done, and you have to take full responsibility for your own life and the current conditions of it. No more mommy, daddy, they, he, she, the community, the world did this or did that. You have to let it go, so that you can move on. You have to understand that the world that you are creating is the world that you desire so everything that will happen within it is based off what you have attracted to it.

So when someone gets on your nerves, you have to dig deep and see why is this person getting on my nerves? What is it about he or she that bothers me so? The reason being is that the person is delivering you a clue about yourself. This is because you attracted them into your world, so obviously they have something for you. Most of us don't want to be honest about who and/or what we are. Many times God sends other people to reflect it upon us in a way that rubs us wrong. This may be to show us who we are currently or to stop us from becoming it later but either way it's something that you need to take notice of. Now, there are some who will just sneakily slide in, but you will be able to recognize them quickly even if they fool you for a minute as something within you will not be able to tolerate them at all for any great amount of time.

How do I actually allow my new reality to unfold?

To allow your new reality to unfold, you have to be in a place of allowance. You have to let it flow. You can't run from the pain or the heartache and quit. You have to just keep pushing through it all. Your pain has great purpose! You have to keep getting up and doing whatever it takes, as you never will know how it will turn out if you stop. You are guaranteed to obtain something great if you continue. Remember one thing leads you to another, so I can't tell you where you are going to end up, but I can definitely tell you that this will get you there. It won't be a quick fix, it won't be something that you brag about and it won't be something that others around you can even understand.

However, it will be great and your life will radically change as well as the experiences within it. It will transform you to become a magnet to attract all that you desire. You will become a wizard at getting what you want, meeting the right people and saying the right things at the right time. You no longer will have to be someone else to get anything, as you will be being you who simply obtains everything. You will be comfortable in setting your boundaries with others, expressing and establishing your beliefs and ideals. You will be compelled to share, as you know your sharing is what will inspire, motivate, encourage, empower, and change the world around you.

So honestly, it is all very simple, it is just that, we as human beings make it hard because we find it difficult to believe in what we cannot see or quantify. The truth is that your greatest gifts and insights are not the ones that are tangible. They are not the cars, the clothes, the degrees, the titles, the mates, and the money. They are your soul, your spirit, your character, your love, your courage, your strength, your faith, your insight, and your beliefs. If you allow these things to lead you, then you will obtain all that you desire because remember your desires are your promises.

They are not just there because you can never have them. They are there because you are supposed to have them; you are supposed to be whom you see yourself as. You have to forget about everything you have learned, and you have to follow your gut to your destiny. The hard part, as discussed before, is getting your mind aligned with the process. As well as building your faith levels up so that you can release the need to control the outcome. Think about it, how many times has your intuition told you to do this or that and you didn't and something bad happened? Think about how many times you said to yourself, I am going to really start following my intuition because x, y, and z?

Also think about how many times you were going to follow your intuition and your mind butted in and gave you a million other reasons why you should do this or that? There is your proof right there; that every time you follow your gut, you make the right choice; every time you let your limited mind talk you out of it, you end up regretting it. There are those of us who choose to live a life of ease or a life of disease. You must decide which one are you going to choose.

How can my new reality unfolding affect others around me?

There are people around you who are affected directly by everything you do or don't do. So if you are living a happier and healthier life, then those people will be beneficiaries of that. If you have a family and you eat healthily, they will, too; if you have a girlfriend and you start working out, she probably will, too; if you have a friend and you're going after your dream career, you will probably inspire him to do the same. Anything that you do that someone else close to you also wants to do will instantly give him/her the momentum to join you. As it's a desire for them, and now through you, it becomes more of a reality. The same is true for bad habits or things that you don't desire anymore.

For better or worse, we all affect the people around us. I always have been very active in my children's lives and very much a part of their overall growth and development. However, for the bulk of my son's memory, I have been mommy, the businesswoman, photographer, radio hostess and community advocate. Therefore, my son only remembered me from the position of being a mover and shaker supermom. He doesn't remember me being simply the great full time mother and wife that I was; this saddened me deeply.

I had to change that, as the truth was, I had been splitting up my time via all those roles therefore, as good of a mom as I was, I knew I could be better. Basically, what I realized was that in gaining my dream, I was giving up the normalcy of my life before the dream. That wasn't the dream at all, because the dream was to have it all. I wanted to be a great community servant, to make money, to be a great mom, to be healthy, to have a good spiritual base, time for friends, and other interests.

The life I was living was all about the work and less about anything else, as it did not allow anything else. Some of you, especially if you are a woman or a single dad, may feel or are going through the same exact situation right now. Yes, you are grateful for the opportunities, but you also know that there are other things that are just as important to you in your life. Why should your career take over the rest of your life? To truly live your best life now, you have to pursue a better quality of life, as a dream career is only one piece to a much larger puzzle.

I know for some of you; you may be thinking, "this all sounds great, but this is big stuff, and there is no way this will work for me." If you are thinking that, then you are absolutely right. This is not for you, as what you believe about you is always the truth. Understand that it is your very own beliefs that set you apart from others. I am sure you probably can shift through your mind, and identify at least one person in your life or that you have come across who has exemplified all that I stated here. You know the type; they are very well liked, their life seems to be great, they get everything they want, they are always happy and upbeat, people are just drawn to them, and things are always working out for them.

If you could switch places with anybody, it would probably be them. So ask yourself, if you can see all of that in them, why can't you see it for yourself? Some people are simply born with this level of insight, and charisma; then there are others who have learned it along the way. Regardless they have the "it" factor and it is what has gotten them where they currently are. This "it" factor is not an exclusive trait as we all have it but most of us do not tap into it.

Some of the things that I have shared with you through this book will be a shock to many who know me, as in their eyes I am the person whom I just asked you to think about. When I walk into a room, I literally take it over and you can feel people's energy dying to be near me. It's not because I am the best looking, the one with the most money, or that I am a celebrity, and everybody knows me. It is because I am confident about who I am, what I believe, what the possibilities of the world are, and my part within it. These things clearly set me apart from everyone else; who deep inside feel small, but on the outside are acting big.

You cannot get caught up in the superficial aspects of life you have to be the realism – no pun intended – that empowers others to exhibit the realism inside of them. I don't walk in a room with fear, doubt, expectation, or an angle. I walk into a room freely adding my gifts and energy to it, while subtracting the gifts and insight that I can gain from it. That level of peace within you radiates unto others and they too desire it. Be the alternative!

CHAPTER SIX

LIVE OUT YOUR NEW REALITY

"Be vulnerable as vulnerability has nothing to do with being weak, and has everything to do with embracing who you are and how you think."

Miguel, Singer-Songwriter & Composer

As I began to implement all of the changes that I desired in my life, I begin to see things completely differently. The peace which I always desired and which was always inside of me begin to wrap me up in a blanket of protection. Things that I feared before were no longer a problem for me. The issues I was having in my life were no longer issues, as they became great opportunities. When I was on my dream journey, I begin to despise certain things, such as cooking and cleaning. I felt as if they were beneath me, as I had more important things to do, like save the world. I much rather would have someone else do all of that, and then complain about how poorly of a job they did. However in my new reality I wanted to be a top chef and a superb house manager.

Basically, I wanted to go back to taking care of my family in those little ways that meant more than the latest pair of sneakers, gadget, or an outing to see the latest movie. You know, those things that we do and buy to compensate for the lack of time and attention that we should really be giving to our children. I wanted my son Shameek, to have memories of me making him nutritious meals daily, that helped his body and mind grow. I wanted to make my mother's famous tuna fish recipe and cut his sandwich in triangular halves. I wanted to give Shameek my full attention as he told me about his day. I looked forward to not being late picking him up but to actually be home when he arrived. I wanted to enjoy staring into his eyes like I did when he was a baby. I just wanted to spend more one on one time with him and do small things that he would remember forever.

Biasia, knew me from this place of sweetness just as Isis knew my mother. However Shameek, at 11 years old never met that woman because he was too young to remember her. I felt like I was cheating him out of a bonding opportunity with me. My daughter Biasia was 16 at this time, and soon she would be going off to college, and my time with her would be limited as well. Biasia and I have always had a great relationship. Although, I am always on her back, as she is an easy going type of person, and I felt that she lacked the go-getter spirit that I had. I desperately wanted Biasia to have that mindset, as I knew how beneficial it was to me. See, even I am guilty of trying to force something into or out of someone based on my own experiences. Ultimately trying to control the outcome for her based on my own standards. Due to this, it definitely caused strain on our relationship, as she grew older.

Biasia, also always seemed to have some level of sadness within her. I constantly addressed this with her, as to me she had no reason to be unhappy. Her life was pretty stable and she wanted for nothing. In addition to that, her family on all sides really poured great amounts of love and attention into her. However, no matter what I did or said, I could never break through Biasia's sadness and later on I found out exactly what it was. My daughter at the age of 14, weeks before her 15th birthday revealed to me that she is a lesbian. Biasia said she was not interested in romantic relationships with the opposite sex, that she suppressed this awareness within herself for years and that she could no longer do it anymore.

There are moments in your life where you will be tested to really see who and what you are made of. These moments are based on the choices that you make, which reveal the true nature of your character. When Biasia, told me about her sexuality, for me, it was one of those major moments. I had to make some tough choices right then and there. These choices were very important, as they would impact the both of us for the rest of our living days. Would I go with my gut and give my child the love, acceptance, and support that she so desperately needed? Or would I go with my mind and turn a blind eye, and tell her that this is just a phase, and she would get over it while continuing to try to stick her in dresses and braids?

I then responded to Biasia, by accepting her truth. Letting her know that I loved her, and that I did not care whom she loved as she would forever be my baby girl, and I would fully support the life that she wanted for herself. I hugged her, and then we started to talk about what would make her feel more comfortable in her own skin and how did she to break the news to her fathers. In that moment, the black cloud that followed my daughter for years was suddenly lifted. It was like a miracle and the sun just came out over her. Biaisa, has never been the same person since. My daughter is now whom she was meant to be, and her light shines so bright as she has showed me as well as many others what true courage looks like.

When Biasia turned 16 and the Sweet Sixteen experiences were over, I was completely drained. I was unexpectedly dramatically, impacted by this milestone in her life. I had no idea that her turning 16 would affect me emotionally and psychologically the way it did. Biasia's, life is a living timeline of my own life; it reveals how far I truly came as an individual. This as well as all of the other circumstances surrounding my life, reflected that God was making it very clear to me that I was at a crossroads. It was time for me to decide whether or not if I was going to keep doing what I was doing, or if I was going to take that next leap of faith to propel my life into the next level of my being.

It made me reflect on who I was, who I used to be, where I wanted to be and whom I wanted to be as well as how much time I really had left to do it. I knew that my current life and its direction would never fulfill me completely as there were so many other concerns that were not being addressed within it. I knew that my children would be out of the house soon. I knew that my current career path was never going to recognize me for my true gifts. I knew that my mindset at that time was limiting my possibilities. I knew that I was not physically healthy, that I was not centered, that I was not spiritually whole, and I knew that there were others in my life that I needed to partner and connect with.

That's when I began to do all of the hard work we spoke about in previous chapters, such as shifting my own reality, searching for answers, finding and implementing them. If I wanted Shameek, to have those experiences; I had to start giving them to him now. If I wanted to spend more time with Biasia in a friendlier rather than mom-the-lecturer way; I had to start doing it now. If I wanted to be more physically fit; I had to start going to the gym, now and if I wanted to make nutritious meals; I had to start shopping for whole foods now. If I wanted to be more spiritually connected; I had to start reading my Bible, other holy books, and many other spiritual resources now. If I wanted to be more centered; I had to begin taking time for myself now, before I decided to give myself to the world. If I wanted to connect and partner with others; I had to make myself available to do that now. Which is exactly what I did.

I begin to make those tuna fish sandwiches I told you about; I started making those great nutritious meals and seeing my family's faces light up as they ate and their bodies grew and shrunk. I started reading the Bible like it was the latest non-fiction New York Times Bestseller, and I was greatly enjoying and learning from it. The Bible is literally the best reality show possible, as it has the greatest amounts of real-life drama. I was relating to many of its characters, especially Abraham and his descendants, as I felt that I was going through the same thing.

I felt like God had hand picked me, to do something great. I gained better understanding of what was happening to me, why it was happening and how to deal with it all. I started hitting the gym, walking the trail, doing yoga, running, and planning to pursue my interest in Zumba, kickboxing, and learning to play my guitar. My body began to change, as I was dropping weight, toning up and my energy levels increased. I started waking up every morning, and not going for my cell phone – which was huge, as most of my work is online. So once I picked up my huge Galaxy Note, then I was all in; being bombarded with the outside world and all of its issues.

What I did start to do to begin my day was become centered, which involved me stretching, praising, praying, and meditating. Then I would give myself some nutritious food, whether that's a full breakfast or simply starting it off with a cup of freshly squeezed, warm lemon juice. The point is all of these things helped me to get strategically centered before I interacted with the rest of the world. So before I started empowering folks, answering questions, responding to emails, dealing with other people and their issues, I would deal with my own. I put myself in a place were I was mentally, physically, and emotionally healthy to assist as well as spiritually grounded so that my assistance would come from God directly and not just me.

As I embarked on starting to live my best life now, I realized two very important factors that would be the foundation of my life for the rest of my days. The first was that I did not have to give up any part of my life for the other, as I did in the past. By that I mean that I did not have to give up my career to take care of my family and friends, and I didn't have to give up my family and friends for my career. However, what I did have to do was set priorities and to maintain balance by managing my time more efficiently, and focusing only on the things that really mattered. The second one was that I was the designer of my days, weeks, and years. I was the boss of my own time.

Therefore I could design my life to be whatever I wanted it to be and accept the consequences and benefits of that. By that I mean that if I only wanted to work half days, then I could do that; now, of course, that means I have less money, but so what? As I could have the rest of my time to spend with family, friends, or doing other things that I enjoy. As I said in chapter one, most of us give money too much credit as we think it's the key to our happiness. The key to our happiness is the quality of our lives that we are leading, and the more tools that we have in our life to manage the task of life, then the easier our lives will be.

For instance, I moved from an urban city to a country suburb, so now I am entrenched in nature. Where I live at the time of this writing is full of trees, animals, flowers, insects, and fresh air, which give me a visual peace beyond my imagination. Every morning, I awake to see myself gently wrapped in blankets of the greenest of green trees that are swaying gentle breezes amongst me. Birds are singing, and sometimes there are dogs barking, but never people yelling, screaming, cursing, or sirens blaring in the air. I look up at the sky, and I have never seen it more beautiful.

I feel blessed to be amongst all of this nature. I am able to enjoy the sun's rays upon me. There are no major catastrophe happening to distract me from these very amazing, but underrated gifts from God. Now does that mean that the world is perfect or my life is perfect? No, it absolutely does not, but what it does mean is that I am having more and more perfect moments. They provide me with a greater sense of appreciation and allows me to be as great as I am with ease.

So with every change that I implement, I gain more and more of my ideal life, and I release more and more of what stands in the way of it. If the news is depressing, simply stop watching it! You really don't have to know about that, as it really has no affect on you in this very moment. If your social media feeds are full of garbage, then shut your account down or unfollow those guys. If whatever you are interacting with is not returning you emotions, information, or results that are geared to your growth and development, then unplug from them. Remember you are the designer of your life, you say what and who goes and stays.

This is how you live your best life now, as you make choices in the present moment that reflect what you want most within it, and you accept the benefits and the consequences of those decisions. You don't get caught up in what others are doing, where they are going, and what they are talking about. You get caught up in what you are doing, where you are going, and what you are talking about. Trust, you will easily find people who reflect your interest as long as you stay true to them. These will be people that everything will unfold easily with because you are both connected to each other by your character rather than by your reputation or superficial ideals.

How can I recognize that my new life is unfolding?

Living your new reality will be challenging at times because again, it's the reprogramming that causes stress. Meaning you will be living it as you are doing it, and you will recognize that it is unfolding as you see that you are doing more of what you want and less of what you don't want. You, too, just as I did, will see your attitude changing and adjusting differently. You will have questions and the answers will flow easily to you in the oddest of ways. However, because you are in a place of allowing, you will be able to recognize these things in yourself and others around you. You will have a sense of self that is clear to you, and you won't be so agitated by things.

You will have high levels of happiness and lower levels of sadness therefore it will be harder for things to infiltrate you and get under your skin. Now, this does not mean in any way that you are bad-day-free for life. Life is full of adversity or challenges everywhere you turn, and what really matters are your reactions to them. When you are living your best life now, you react differently most times because your happiness is more important than your ego's need to be right. You also become more aware of your emotions, so you know when you are not feeling well and don't really want to be bothered.

Instead of the old you who would push through and have a miserable time anyway. You will opt to stay home; knowing that it is better to take care of yourself and make sure you don't ruin anybody else's time. You will be aware when you are out of the living-your-best-life-now zone and you will know what you need to get yourself back on track.

The more changes you implement, the more your life will reflect your desired vision. You will know when it completely has unfolded, when your life is being easily what it is that you desired for it to be. Throughout every chapter I spoke to you about how hard this process will be, but when you get to this point, the process is no longer a process. It is no longer hard as it's simply a way of life. It is the way in which you live your life; the people in your life are different, you are different, the relationships that you had before your changes are different. Your life is no longer a challenge in of itself. It is more of the way in which things are, as if they have been like that forever. Soon enough you will be so improved that you don't even remember the ways of your old self.

You will be clear on why all the things of the past happened, and you will be so busy living the good life that you won't care about the issues of the past. You will be so focused on planning for the future while living joyfully in the present. You will enjoy your moments in life rather than being focused on when the next one is unfolding. The simple things that you never paid attention to will now be the greatest things ever; such as reading a book, biting into a strawberry, or seeing two little kids playing together. You will amaze yourself of how grateful you will be, and the level of joy that you will feel. Happiness is not simply a fleeting emotion – it is an attitude and a way of life based off of the truth within of you.

Most only feel happiness at certain times, like holidays, births, and getting something they wanted. Ironically, many people choose to do the exact opposite of what their happiness demands. By this I mean, they don't want to go somewhere, but they go; they don't want to do something, but they do it; they really want this, but they settle for that and then they expect you to do the same thing. Not me. If I don't want to do it, then I am not doing it, and I don't care if that pisses you off. As to me that is your problem and that's not me being stubborn, that's me loving me. Why should someone suffer for someone else?

That's not love; that is sick and controlling. I would rather someone tell me no, then to sit there and do it, but really don't want to. Don't poison my drink with your negative energy, as it just makes the whole experience the worst for everybody. You didn't want to do it in the first place, so you didn't do it right or lovingly. I can sense all that, and your attitude behind it does not leave space for me to truly appreciate your efforts, so at the end nobody wins. However, in your new reality that should not be the case, as you will not participate in the things of the world that you do not appreciate. You will clearly understand for yourself that whatever you magnify, you manifest.

How can I deal with others from my old reality not liking or understanding me?

When it comes to the people from your past, they simply fall in one or two categories; the people that matter and the people that don't. For the people that don't matter, like distant friends, colleagues, and even fans at times, depending on who you are and what type of life you are leading you just shut them out. Simply let them go. The reason that they don't matter is not because they are unworthy, but they don't bring any great value to your life so you don't need them. Now if you have fans of some sort, this can be a little gray area, rather than black or white, because, of course, your fans are important to you, and have helped you to get where you are. I can talk about this, because I, too, have fans, and with today's social media, plenty of ordinary people have fans, so fans are no longer just for celebrities. We all take our fans seriously because they do support us in one way or another. However, if they are true, then they will stick with you, and if they are not, then show them the door too. You can't live your life for them. You always have to live your life for you and for God first.

This book for me is also being used as a way to transition my current audience into accepting the new but old me. While also introducing and attracting those into my life who currently are or wish to be living their best life now. By this I mean, it lets them know that I haven't abandoned them, and I didn't fall off the wagon. I'm just going into a new a direction and I hope that it's one that they are willing to come along with. If they are not, well, that's ok too. I say the new but old me because this may be new to them, but it's old to me as it's who I always was, and it's the very reasoning behind why I did the things I did. I only want people in my network who are about this life.

One of my current challenges as I write this is to extract those who are about start living your best life now, and to subtract those from my audience who are not. You must understand that the importance is not based off of the quantity of people in your life or your network it is based off of the quality of people that matter. So you can have 100 followers, and if those 100 followers are engaged totally and supportive, then you got a great tribe. This is much better than having 10,000 or 100,000 followers who don't support you, and you are not even interested in their stuff either. Those who follow the crowd only go as far as the crowd goes and those who walk alone find themselves in places never known.

For the people who do matter, like family, mates, and true friends, you will have to be a little more patient in their ability to adjust to the new you. For family and friends, meaning mom, dad, brothers, sisters, children and besties, they should be accepting of your new changes, and they also should be happy for you, as these are the people who support you no matter what. They are the ones who ultimately just want you to be happy. However, depending upon whatever your changes are, it may not be so easy and by that I mean for some of you this book may help you to come out of the closet about something. You might be ready to tell your family that you are gay or that you are in love with someone whom they may frown upon, or your mate that you want a divorce. Whatever it is at the end of it all, you have to be true to yourself.

If the people who say they love you really do more than they want to be right or comfortable, then they will accept you for who you are or you will have to accept them for who they are, and let them go. Now, I know that it's much easier to say than to do, but at the end of the day, that's what it is. When it comes to even more serious relationships, like your husband or wife, you have to do everything in your power to get them to understand and participate in your growth and development. If they do not, and it is not working, and you see that you are no longer compatible with each other, then you have to move on with your life.

There is no need to be imprisoned by anyone, especially a mate. Your mate's importance is the highest relationship as an adult outside of God that you can have. Your entire being is wrapped up in theirs, and if they are not on the same wavelength as you, then there is no possible way that you can start living your best life now with them as they will be a constant blocker and knocking you out of the zone.

How will living my new reality impact others?

Now with all of that being said, it does not mean that they completely have to be out of your life. For some it will just mean that their role is changing, like when I told you about my sister girlfriend Nicole. In my old reality, she was my best friend, and in my new reality, she is simply my sister; no less than my biological ones. The reason being is that her gifts were more in the sister zone rather than in the best friend one. She is still a very significant part of my life, that now brings me much more joy rather than any pain. Living your new reality will impact people greatly! You will be like the magical bees and beautiful flowers of life. Most people fear bees, and many people don't stop to bask in the enjoyment of a beautiful flower.

These two universal gifts in our society are the very foundation of how we live. If they did not do the work that they do, our lives would be completely different or non-existent. Most of us are totally oblivious to their functions, and how grateful we should be to them for it. See, bees eat pollen and nectar from flowers, and as they gather it for themselves, they also spread it unto other flowers. This activity makes more flowers by crosspollination, which in turn makes more food produced from plants. That we then, as human beings eat. It has been said that one out of every three bites of food that you eat depends on a honeybee. So, the next time you see one, don't be so quick to kill it out of fear that it is going to sting you; just get away.

Bringing this back to the question at hand, what I am saying is that you too, just like a bee, will discretely bring harmony and healing among the earth. I continue to say the same thing chapter after chapter when it comes to this, because I want you to clearly understand that your life is not just about you! You have an important role to play and simply by living your life in the greatest way possible, which means expressing your true gifts and blessing your neighbors with your smiles and energy, will in itself assist in bringing and keeping peace on earth. You may not be the guy or gal who gets the awards, who gets on TV, and your name may not be the one put in the history books, but your life will matter.

Understand that in the laws of the universe, there is no one thing or person of greater or lesser value. We all have a role to play in keeping this thing that we call life going. At this day and age in the 21st century, we are the pioneers of a new humanity. There is a transformation in human consciousness taking place and you are going to be on the leading edge of that. It's like being one of the first people to know about the Internet and your ideas are the very foundation of how we are using technology today. Start Living Your Best Life Now folks are about evolving themselves, as individuals of the human species, so that the world can transform itself into a place where love triumphs over fear and awareness triumphs over ignorance. You must be the very you that the world needs.

In doing so you will transform it from the inside out. That's what is so amazing about this, as it has significant benefits for you, others around you, and mankind in general. I know as we approach the end of this book, and every chapter I probably start to scare some of you with this world stuff. However, just remember that the world in itself, just like your life, is not complete. Even though some of the things that I am saying may be way ahead of you right now; you really have nothing to lose by trying it. I am not telling you to go out and save the world. I am encouraging you to save yourself, and I am making it clear to you that by doing that one act, you will help heal the world.

Also take a moment and consider where your skepticism may be coming from. Is that your gut saying, "she is crazy" or is that your mind? I can tell you right now that if you are having any doubts about anything that I am saying, it is coming from your mind. Your mind is saying; "you can't do that, you're too old, you're too young, you're too deep into that relationship, you will be alone, you can't quit your job, how will you survive, she/he doesn't really love you, and who do you think you are?" Your spirit is saying, "yes, it's the truth, listen to her, I have been trying to tell you all along, you can do this, you want to do this, follow your dream, and the moment is right now." However, your spirit's voice sounds like a whisper, while your mind's voice is as clear as another person speaking to you.

The reason why you are hearing those voices the way that you are is because we have been trained to use our minds and to suppress our feelings. We have been told that our ability to reason or rather have logic is what makes us superior beings, and that's true when related to other life forms, such as animals, but the buck stops there. As I told you before, the mind is very often the devil's advocate because again, it is limited to logic, and experience. As it interprets information, it searches like Google through these two tunnels trying to make sense of it all. If it has no point of reference, then the mind goes blank, and tells you that something is wrong, not true, and/or cannot be done.

However, where our mind stops you must remember our spirits begin. Your spirit is the non-physical part of your being that is the seat of your soul, and it is where your emotions and your true character live. The knowledge and understanding that your spirit has surpass your mind and anything that you could possibly think of. This is the part of you that is directly connected to the creator of all things; God. So, the instruction that you receive from it is the most trusted instruction that you will ever receive from anything. You don't have to believe me, as I am not trying to convince you.

I will tell you that for better or worse, you were meant to read this, just as I was meant to write it. Don't listen to me, listen to your spirit as you read and reread the words that I am saying. Your spirit alone will tell you whether this information is for you or not. If it resonates, then it is for you at this time; if it does not, then that's ok, too, because it is not for you at this time. Either way you go, just make sure it's with your gut, as it will always take you where you are supposed to be. The one who followed his mind, got lost and the one who followed his spirit, found himself.

CHAPTER SEVEN

HONOR YOUR CURRENT REALITY FOR WHAT IT IS AND FOR WHAT IT WILL BRING

"You have to create your own lane to make it what it will be, and decide that you are good enough."

Marsha Ambrosius, Singer-Songwriter

After moving and applying all the changes that I could in my new reality, I started to feel great again about the direction that my life was headed. I felt a sense of extreme accomplishment, because I now was taking charge of my life in a holistic way. I had a new direction for my career, and I was implementing strategies and getting great results. My family was totally supportive and involved in my work. The children were adjusting very well into their new atmosphere, and we were becoming even closer as a family. When we moved, we had a few friends and a couple of family members throughout the state, but it was still pretty much just the four of us. This isolation was a great thing at the time, because we all needed to adjust and focus on our new lives in the south. My husband and I were learning more and more about each other daily, and I personally was doing my best to have no secrets between us.

I begin to find myself going deeper and deeper into a spiritual journey of my own. I found myself searching for answers and understanding for certain things that happened in my life that I had no control over, although they were still present in my mind, body and spirit. One answer lead me to another, which calmed my spirit from feeling anxiety, however, it also awakened it further. My spirit started to tell me things I really did and didn't want to know, and it started to show me things that I really did and didn't want to see. For the things that I did want to know and see, I was happy to have some level of understanding about them that I did not have before. The reason why I didn't want to know or see some of the other things was because they were things I could not do anything about, therefore I felt powerless and imprisoned by them.

As time went on, I dealt with them by accepting the fact that there was much more to my life that I never would know about until it happened. I also realized that as blessed as I was to receive great insight from God, at the end of the day I too am a spiritual being having a human experience that involves some level of conformity. God knows what's best for all of us, and He knows when to give us what. Most times we are not ready to receive all that He has for us. It's like those crazy lottery stories you hear about, where somebody wins millions, and are flat broke in a couple of years. In your mind, you are probably like, "that would have never been me, because I would have done this or done that," but the reality is, that could be any one of us.

You never know what you will do or how you would respond if given everything you ever wanted at one time or at least access to it. The point I am making is that life is a series of stages and plateaus, and like I told you before, once you reach one level there will be another, and so forth. So, as you transform your life into the direction and the reality you desire, understand that the process never actually stops, as you will find more that needs to be corrected or ejected. You have to be patient for what you don't have now. While putting the work into obtain it, and being optimistic about receiving it later.

In the meantime and in-between time, you have to maintain an attitude of gratitude for all the greatness that you do have in your life at the present moment. This might not sound like much, but this is the key to your sanity and your abundance. An attitude of gratitude is when you are beyond grateful for all that you have, while still planning and preparing for the more that you desire. Many of us live our lives focusing on what we do not have and we allow it to control our overall perspective.

You can have a million things in your life going right, but those 10 things that are not have your main attention and energy. We have to reverse this, as that attitude is where many of us lose our souls. Remember, there is more to life than increasing its speed, as if you receive and know everything, then what's the point of living for the next 70 years? I say this to say that the more you live, you grow, and the more you search and find answers, the more your life will change, expand and increase.

So none of us are ever really there yet, including myself, but with God's help and ideals like Start Living Your Best Life Now, we do get closer and closer day by day. Life is a journey, and it's about enjoying that journey through exploration, growth and development. This means experiencing pain, obstacles, joys, hardships, triumphs, confusion, love, tragedy, and being challenged beyond disbelief. Each day you should be better than your last. Yes, you still will have hard days, but you will be able to manage them better as well as get back up on the horse faster. You will awake with many more days of feeling accomplished rather than feeling like something is missing and you could be doing more.

The reason for this is that you must understand that all the things that happen to you in your life, for better or worse, are in your best interest. These experiences are helping you become the very you that you were meant to be. If you are currently going through hell, just keep going, in the end you will understand why. Therefore, quitting is never an option when it comes to living.

So after all of that growth and development, my next move on my journey was to actually write this book, which I challenged myself to do it in 7 days. As I write this final chapter on the seventh day, I am quite proud to say that I did it! Now, of course, I have to go back, do several rewrites, have my editor edit it and then review it a million more times, but overall the meat and potatoes are here. I did it while being extremely sick for five of the seven days. Kudus to me! I share this with you, because I hope that you can be inspired by my life, my challenges, my journey, and what is yet to come.

If I could face and overcome all of my junk and my life is nowhere near over, complete, or perfect, then you most certainly can to. The truth is; I really didn't write this book, I just was the instrument used by God to pen it. This book unbeknownst to me has been in the making for 33 years. That's why I could get it all out so quickly because all I did was follow my gut and He did the rest. When you find the courage within to change your perception, then God will change your reality. If there is a will inside of you, then God will make a way. The more that you recognize who you really are the less you are willing to be who you were or who you are not. Even the writing of this book was emotionally difficult and a very deep journey in itself.

I am sure to suffer some consequences from people's opinions about this or that. I am also sure that some who are mentioned may have a problem about what I said about them, why did I say what I said or why did I put that into the book etc. However, it's my story from my perspective and for me to start living my best life now I had to take the risk and just tell it all. I tried my best to negotiate and cooperate in the relationships I spoke about, I went above and beyond for the benefit of others and I never received anything in return but a whole lot of heartache and pain and I refuse to do it any longer.

I will not cry in silence to protect the truth and secrets of others whom choose to be less than what their life is offering. I am cleaning out the closets in my life to make space for all that is yet to come. Some maybe offended by that, however that is something they will have to deal with. I have heard too many times from people I have loved and served that "I didn't ask you to do that and you don't need to do that for me" so Start Living Your Best Life Now is my response.

Life is to interesting to be made up. So hopefully you can use mine as a guide for your own. Life is about choices and you have to choose who you want to be and how you want to live. I want to live greatly and that means accepting all that comes with life; the good, the bad and the ugly. I do not hide in the face of life as death will take us all one day and when that day happens for me it is my greatest desire to go in peace with no regrets.

I want you to know that I don't have it all together, but

the difference between me, and most is that I am actively pursuing it. Like I told you in the last chapter, I know what I know and I know that the information I gave you here is the information you need to go from point A to point B, and then from point B to point C, and on and on. Understand it's only a beginning, a push in the right direction from someone who has been there and done that.

Through my own personal hardships, this book was born, and not because I know everything, but because I have learned from what I have experienced. Now, most of the time when someone writes a book like this, or has this level of insight as I do, they never say, I don't know it all, or my stuff is not all together, but I am sure as you can see by now, I am not like most. Perfection is not my goal, but truth and understanding are my mission. I am just like you, a regular human being, making it through life, who has something to share. In this book, I do use my story, and I am the one writing these thoughts down, but they are not mine. As I told you before, I am simply a messenger with a message. This message will either resonate with you because it's for you or it won't because it is not but either way you will not be able to say that nobody ever told you.

Even Your Pain Has Great Purpose

I hope this book has been as insightful for you to read as it has been for me to write. My overall goal in life is to assist people as well as myself on the path to living at their absolute highest potential. Although as I write this, I am extremely clear that I am not there yet, I am even more aware that I am on my way. I have been married for seven years, and I have been linked at the heart with Greg for 20 years altogether and four years ago I met MT.

At the time of our unexpected meeting, I was already knee-deep in marital differences with Greg but still semi-content.

Unbeknownst to me at the time this mere fact put me in a place of allowing. By that I mean that if I was not going through the things I was going through with Greg, I never would have heard God, when He told me to pay attention to MT. The reason being is because I truly loved my husband, and when things were great, they were beyond great, and I never had a wandering eye or heart. However, this man changed me upon meeting him as he consumed my heart in the time that it took to say hello, and I have never been the same person since.

Meeting MT was like finding something that I never knew I lost. Our very unconventional relationship as well as all of the confusion and pain it has caused me is the very reason I have come to so much understanding in my life. It is also the main reason I decided to start living my best life now. He unexplainably awoken things inside of me that I never knew existed. His energy became keys to the doors of my life. To make this even stranger our relationship is one of a spiritual nature, as it has never went any further than what I shared. We have never been intimate, we rarely ever spent any time together, he too is now married, and I am a thousand miles away.

Although none of this has ever weakened our bond so much so that I can always feel his energy with me. The physical distance between us exists for many reasons but the most important and obvious one is so that we can live out our experiences with those whom we love and that came before either of us. I know he and Greg both will be greatly affected that I have revealed all of this. However, I have carried this burden in silence for to long and for my own sanity, I will no longer do it for either of them.

We both seem to have an underlying but weird understanding that neither of us are ready to take on the responsibility of the other. As well as our connection is so intense that if a union is made during these times, it has the potential to possibly destroy us both. A modern day Romeo and Juliet story on the surface, but when you look deeper, we are more like Isis and Osiris. I was going to leave this all out of the book to protect Greg and MT, but I could not do so in good conscience. This whole situation has been killing me for years now and both of them are strikingly oblivious to it.

By that I mean no matter what I say to either one of them they both act as if I am some astronomical superhuman who doesn't feel and will just get over it. As if it causes no stress and that I am just going to be ok. Even when I painfully make it clear that I am not ok; neither of them listens. Therefore to continue living my best life now I have to do what is best for me per God's instruction. Letting go is my current task; I can no longer overzealously love people who are incapable of loving me properly. If people don't see or are too afraid to receive the opportunity you are providing them then that's their loss. This goes back to when I spoke to you earlier about the Play-Doughing of relationships. Just don't do it; remember ease not disease.

Love for me has never been easy, as every man that I have loved has always made me work to prove it. For some reason they never believed that I truly had an interest in them. I believe this is a reflection of their insecurity, as they must of thought that I was something pretty special in which they themselves did not deserve. I did have one lover; Muhammad, who loved me so greatly in all the ways that I needed to be loved. Now when

Muhammad actualized in my life it was after I broke up with Lawrence, I was already pregnant and my heart had always been with Greg so he never really had the opportunity that he truly deserved. He loved me unconditionally for years on end and never missed a moment to share it. However, we were young and because of all the matters I was dealing with I never recognized the full multitude of or returned his love in the way he gave it. I treated him more like a friend and not the lover that he really was.

It took me years to really understand how and why I treated him the way that I did. As well as how he could keep loving me regardless but I understand now. Muhammad was a gift from God as he protected and provided for me at a time when I needed it. Unbeknownst to me at the time, he revealed to me the type of love my being truly needs in the manners in which it needs it. Although I was completely blinded to those facts then but I am forever grateful to him for it now. Muhammad is the only man who made it clear in both good times and bad that he felt worthy of me and was the only man through action and deed willing to do whatever it took by any means to have me.

The reason why I am compelled to reveal all my truth to you especially the part of it that has propelled me to this very moment in my life is because I am still working on it. This love situation has violently plagued my heart, my mind, my body, and my soul for years now. However, if for not these troubling circumstances, this book would not exist at this time, and the ideals of Start Living Your Best Life Now would probably still be buried within the depths of my subconscious. Therefore even your pain has great purpose, as it will take you places you could never imagine. However, you must brace yourself to receive the gift within your storms as if not conscious about such truth you will give them the ability to break you.

You see, I am a very honest person, and I do not believe in wasting opportunities to tell people that I love what they need to hear, even if they don't like it. I choose to live my life free from regrets or unfinished business as none of us are actually promised tomorrow. I don't believe in delaying the truth because of discomfort. I know that all things are in God's mighty hands, that His timing is the best timing, and that His will is far greater than the individual desires of our hearts. Therefore, it is not easy for me to disregard the fact that it is time to let go of my marriage and it is equally time to let go of this metaphysical love.

I cannot and do not want to hide the truth that my marriage has come to a beautiful end and not because of another man, but because it is time. Endings are not sad for those who know that for every end there is a beginning. I cannot and do not want to hide the truth that I have love for someone. Love is a good thing and Love is God. So damn the man who shames love. In today's society love is the most revolutionary thing that we can possibly do right now. So while I am in control, of working out, making those tuna fish sandwiches, deciding who and what I want in my life, and uplifting others, I, just like you are not in control of the way in which God teaches us.

These situations reflect residue from my past and evidence of my future. It is all God's will. The understanding for all of us involved will probably come later if ever. For better or worse, I will always submissively move according to God's plan. Right now God's plan is for me to be patient, for me to be strategic, and for me to take action on the things that I can, and to be still on the matters that I cannot do anything about.

To really honor your reality, you must first be honest about it. I will not live in silence any longer about how I am feeling and what I am going through. Understand that God's call will disrupt your life because it is meant to do so. Yes, this truth does hurt others, but it also gives life. When I told Greg that I was in love with another man and my heart was not with him; it was less than a perfect situation. It was not planned, and the reaction became heated, but it just spilled out. I had no idea that when we went out to eat that evening that it would end with me saying this four days before our seventh marriage anniversary. I also did not know that a few days later that I would become so enraged with MT that I sent him a hate-filled correspondence. Totally emasculating him with the purpose of evoking pain, simply because I was in my pain and that's how I truly felt about him. By way of those circumstances, I have come to the understanding that the truth simply was that I had eruptively evolved. Enough was enough, it was the closing of a door and an opening of another.

I was no longer the young girl that Greg fell in love with or the lost woman that MT awakened. To continue walking in my purpose and to fully live my best life now, I had to let the lost girl of 13 go; who lives only in the heart of Greg. I also had to let the lost young woman of 29 go; who lives only in the mind of MT. Yes, to some, it may sound horrible to some degree. Once you get over the initial shock, you will see that this is real life and a few things are happening. The first is I am free from hiding such important facts from the people whom I love, which was keeping a certain amount of distance between us.

Also, this is not a complete shock for Greg, as he knew

about MT for some time now and we already decided on the divorce, because of our very own matters. Understand this is not a situation where I am getting a divorce or leaving my husband for another. This is a mutual decision between my husband and I, because we are no longer compatible as husband and wife. Greg is beyond a phenomenal man in his own right, and we have come as far as we can with each other in these roles. Our next levels of growing require our removal from the current positions that we are in.

By this I mean, when you truly love a person you understand that loving them is about doing what is in the best interest of them, even when they don't agree or it hurts you greatly. For MT, he now knows the whole truth about how I feel about him overall. I have finally revealed to him the other side of my feelings in regards to his actions as well as the consequences of them. For me, I am clear at this time that I must move on with my life without either of them drowning me with their issues that prevent them from loving me properly.

Providing the space that we all need so that we as individuals may hear from God more loudly. I will begin my hardest challenge yet to date, which is the ability to truly let go. Seeking God's friendship and to trust more fully, as He is always with me, and I must accept and appreciate that. If I ever thought that I was alone, I was wrong, as with God, I am never alone. The physical presence of other humans beings although extremely comforting will never lead you to living your best life. This is because most are afraid to live their own, let alone encourage or support you to.

For me to continue to start living my best life now, I must let go of both Greg and MT in the ways in which I have been holding them. They both tirelessly distract me with disappointment and pain for many different reasons. More importantly, by letting go of them I let go of my old selves. Greg and I have spoken about and attempted divorce in the past, as we were separated, and living separately for two years at one point. We also obtained the divorce papers at that time, but God knew we were not ready, as we were not in a place of complete understanding.

The time has come, and we both have accepted the fact that our relationship simply comes down to us both growing up and apart. We are no longer as we used to be, our needs have changed, our spiritual contract in this manner have come to an end. The best and most loving thing we can do for the other is to let each other go. We are no longer the children who fell in love, as we are now the adults who need to be loved in specific ways that we are both incapable of doing for the other.

If we are to remain the loving beings, best friends and family that we are to each other, then we both must be honest and responsible in preserving our respect, appreciation, love, and friendship for the other. I know this will sadden many who know us, but these are the types of hard decisions that one must make to start living your best life now. This is what people who truly love each other do, as they handle their responsibilities, and they protect the people they love by being honest.

My husband and I have shared over 20 years of our lives together, and we are both only in our early 30s. Stop and imagine how truly blessed we actually are. As we have grown up together, we directly have assisted in the development of one another. Each of us has directly contributed to the person that we are today, and we have so many memories as well as our children to always represent the love that we share. Our love has not ended in flames. We do not hate each other or despise one another, as it is our great friendship that gives us strength in these very trying times. Greg is and has always been my best friend, we have taken the world together and nothing can ever come in between that or be more important than that. I will die loving this great man and I will do whatever it takes to preserve our great relationship which is much more important than our marriage.

No one is leaving the other, and no one has come between us, therefore this is not a sad story; it is a new chapter for both of us in our lives. Greg has been a great asset to me; he has provided, protected, and loved me to the best of his ability as well as he is beyond an amazing father. You must understand that when God calls you, nothing, and I mean nothing, can hold you. I have not only been called, but I have answered and it requires me to be, do, and think in ways that are unconventional to most. Trust, the situation is very difficult. However, we are making it and learning the practice of unconditional love in the process.

As I told you before, to Start Living Your Best Life Now you will be confronted by some of the toughest decisions and experiences of your lifetime. Regardless, you must honor the journey and let your inner being guide you. No man can interfere with God's will or he will find himself broken and beaten. I must continue following my gut. As it guides me into places that I am afraid to go I remain in absolute faith. As they say, the sun will come out tomorrow and I say when it rains, things grow, people change, and places are made better.

I have no idea from this point on what will happen between MT and I. Although, I would be lying if I did not say that I would enjoy exploring and experiencing his love in a more tangible way. I always felt that he was directly connected to my soul and a great key to my destiny. However, I also have acknowledged the possibility that this experience in itself maybe the full actualization of such truth. Revealing at this great moment in time that the gift has been given and received therefore this is as far as it goes for us. Sometimes we can become so distracted by the gift's bearer that we forget who the gift is actually from.

Either way, I am beyond grateful to him and I have done my part per God's instruction. We have something unexplainably significant between us, and he loves me in a peculiar manner. A love that makes me feel he is operating in the best interest of me as if he knows something that I don't, or that he is merely being cowardice and will live a lifetime of regret. God brought us together for a reason, and if it was for this awakening within, and nothing more; than that in itself is worth a million loves in a million lifetimes.

Regardless of which, for me at this time, it is in my best interest to stand still. I clearly understand that only MT can decide or determine for himself, if he is living his best life now. I now understand and accept that the connection between us has always been a matter that is out of my hands. You have to make space for God to do his work and sometimes it is not meant for you to understand. So trying to gain understanding when you should just be allowing will cause you to be distraught and it will push the very things that you desire away. I have hurtfully learned throughout my life that you cannot control everything and at times the desire to control can be the very thing blocking you from all that you need.

Without any expectation from neither of the leading men in my life or plans, at this time I choose to honor my new reality by staying true to it, and focusing on doing what's best for me. No matter how hard it is, no matter whom it disappoints, and no matter what others feel or think about it. I am determined as you should be, as well, to always live your best life now by being all that God has deemed you to be in every moment, in every second, and in every hour of each day by any means necessary.

In my external relationships whether platonic or romantic, I, just as you deserve to be loved properly within them. I will no longer fight for this love as it should be lovingly given and if not then it is something that I can do without. As I end this I am beyond grateful that the ideals of "Start Living Your Best Life Now" has pushed me this forward in my life. Yes it is extremely difficult, but it is all being addressed. There is an ending and a beginning to all that is current and all that will come to past. We are not in charge of our lives, as we have all come here with a job to do, and our job is to simply live it out. Living comes with pain, takes courage and is full with both joy and excitement.

Your most important obligation in life is to be who God designed you to be, as you have great purpose no matter how subtle your impact is. So in my knowing that, I willing sacrifice my being throughout these pages for the betterment of yours. Don't think I am not afraid to share all of this; to be judged, to wonder who am I hurting or embarrassing, to deal with who is going to be mad at me, to carry the weight of others and to ponder about what are my friends going to think, but I am compelled to do it. If I am going to please anyone than it has to be God.

If you notice, I have spoken about God throughout this entire text, and it is because all glory goes to him. It is He who has led both you and I to this exact moment in time, and it is He who will lead both you and I to the next and the next. However, if we ignore, if we fear, if we hate, and if we allow our ego to lead us, then we widen the gap between God and us. We prolong the turmoil within our life, and we remain blinded to the possibilities of actualizing our very own greatness.

Use my story as a guide for yours, use my pain as comfort for your own, and use my truth as courage to tell your own. Whatever you do, just do something. Start living your best life now doesn't mean everything always will be great or easy, but it means you are willing to go the distance, so that you may be whom God has destined you to be. I was meant to experience all that I did, all that I will, and all that I am going through now, so that I can bring forth the gifts of insight, understanding, empathy, courage, and truth. So I willingly obliged, sharing with you my past, present, and future adversities to let you know that I, just as you can, have chosen to keep standing, smiling, helping, giving, and living greatly!

Start Living Your Best Life Now Against All Odds

You must understand that you celebrate and honor your best life by adhering to the tools, tips, and techniques that got you there in the first place. You learn to listen to God when He speaks and you learn to respond to the calls no matter how difficult they are. As mentioned before, these are the things that allow your life to unfold, as it should. This produces great joy for you, because you are in alignment with all that you are and all that you should be. I share my pain with you, because I want you to see that the processes of living your best life now is continuously evolving. As long as you have breath, you will face adversity, and as long as you have will, you should choose to start living your best life now in the face of it.

I shared my entire story, especially the greatest drama in my life that plagues me now and forces me to put the information set forth in this book to work overtime. As well as it is the very reasoning to how such book has come to life, so that you can become inspired and enlightened to understand that you cannot control all things. You must be the defining factor in your very own life. You must not fear the unknown and the hardship, as you must pursue with vigor your best life in the face of any circumstance, as you only have one chance to get it right and it's now.

I have learned everything I said to you in this book, because of one heartbreaking circumstance that pulled my whole life together like a puzzle. I shared it with you because I wanted you to know that life is not easy for any of us and that we all are always struggling with areas in our lives that we wish were different. I could have omitted this part of the story, but that would have been cowardly, and it would not have helped the people who just read it and became inspired or directed to take an action concerning their own situations.

As I stated to you in an earlier chapter, the hardest part about all of this is making the decision to commit, but you have nothing to lose and everything to gain. The greatest part is that by challenging yourself to be the best you possible, then you simultaneously assist with bringing peace on earth. Living your dreams simply means to do what you want, when you want, how you want, and with whom you want. Therefore, this reality is not out of your reach, and it is not something that you have to wait until your next lifetime to have. This is your life now, and for better or worse, you are always creating your own reality. It's just that up until this point you either didn't know it, or you, like me, allowed outside influences to dictate it.

When I say to stop living by default and to start living on purpose, what I am saying to you is to turn up your conscience, follow your gut, begin listening to it, and for better or worse, let it guide you. Stop just accepting whatever attaches itself to you, feeling like you have no control over the people, places, and things within your existence. Stop inviting the junk into your life by settling for less, and then reacting to it. Stop secretly imprisoning yourself by the limitations of your circumstances. Start living in a creative mode where you are freely and lovingly dictating the who, what, when, and where in your life, in real time, based only upon what you truly desire.

Remember, you can do this as you were born to do it, and nobody deserves it more than you! Like the old saying says, "get up, get out, and get into it." Your best life is waiting on the other side of everything you don't want, and your job is to clear the clutter. The more junk you remove on the inside and the outside of you, the more possibilities and opportunities you will see. You either are going to get rid of something or excitedly jump right into it, but that's it and that's your measuring stick.

It's time to clean your internal closet and what is good you keep, and what is bad you throw away! Ask yourself; is this a person, place, or thing that I increase from, or is this a person, place, or thing that I decrease from? It is very simple; all you have to do is make the decision to do it, stick with it, and go under, above, or around any obstacle that stands in your way.

Honestly speaking, you do this all the time, just on a much smaller level. Those new shoes you got, either you bought them on sight, or you planned to get them, but either way, you saw them, you wanted them, and you got them. The same thing happened with the car you are driving; the apartment, the house, or condo you are living in; the man or woman that you are with; the cell phone you have; and all the other gadgets, clothes, food, events, people and places that you have bought and removed in and out of your life.

You have to simply shift and sift through the things that are not serving you well, you have to fight for what you want and let go of what you don't. You have to appreciate all that you have, in the mean time, while preparing and planning for what is ahead. You must be strong and patient, as God knows what and when. You have to honor and respect all that you have experienced and will continue to experience, as that is how you celebrate your now.

You must acknowledge and appreciate the journey of where you were, where you are, and where you are going. The more you understand and apply such understanding, the more you receive and the easier your life will be as you truly are the constant creator of our own reality. The only thing great enough to stand in-between where you are now and where you want to be is you. So, make up your mind; are you going to keep wishing things were differently, or are you going to Start Living Your Best Life Now and make them different?

About the Author

Realism Hargrave, specializes in the business of living. As a Life Coach, Author and Motivational Speaker with an extensive background in Media, Marketing & Communications she empowers individuals and organizations to transform their lives and enhance their performance. Realism's Start Living Your Best Life Now philosophy is to provide you with the necessary inspiration, knowledge, support and training you need to bring out the absolute best in you. She challenges your ideals, expands the possibilities within your life and increases your performance levels by encouraging you to discover and remove the distractions & stumbling blocks.

If you are looking for a dynamic Speaker to address your organization and enhance work life performance or 1 on 1 coaching to transform the life you are living into the one you are desiring than for more information please visit www.realismhargrave.com.

You can contact Realism Hargrave directly at

rh@realismhargrave.com & connect with her in real time

on Facebook, Instagram and Youtube. @RealismHargrave

"Don't just wish things were differently, make them different." -RH

Made in the USA
Lexington, KY
10 March 2014